MASTERING
MONEY

Napoleon Hill (1883–1970), best known for his global bestseller *Think and Grow Rich*, was a self-help author and businessman whose work has influenced millions across the world.

James Allen (1864–1912) retired from the business world to pursue a lifestyle of contemplation and wrote many books, including *As a Man Thinketh* and *The Path of Prosperity*.

Roger Fritz (1928–2011) was an American management consultant and the author of over 63 self-help and management development books, including *The Power of a Positive Attitude* and *What Managers Need to Know*.

MASTERING MONEY

How to Become Rich

RUPA

Published by
Rupa Publications India Pvt. Ltd 2024
7/16, Ansari Road, Daryaganj
New Delhi 110002

Sales centres:
Bengaluru Chennai
Hyderabad Jaipur Kathmandu
Kolkata Mumbai Prayagraj

Edition copyright © Rupa Publications India Pvt. Ltd 2024

All rights reserved.
No part of this publication may be reproduced, transmitted,
or stored in a retrieval system, in any form or by any means, electronic,
mechanical, photocopying, recording or otherwise, without the prior
permission of the publisher.

P-ISBN: 978-93-5702-774-8
E-ISBN: 978-93-5702-661-1

First impression 2024

10 9 8 7 6 5 4 3 2 1

Printed in India

This book is sold subject to the condition that it shall not, by way of
trade or otherwise, be lent, resold, hired out, or otherwise circulated,
without the publisher's prior consent, in any form of binding or
cover other than that in which it is published.

CONTENTS

1. Visions and Ideals — 7
   James Allen
2. How Attitude Affects Results — 14
   Roger Fritz
3. Self-Control — 56
   Napoleon Hill
4. Organized Planning — 69
   Napoleon Hill
5. Positive Mental Attitude — 93
   Napoleon Hill
6. Transcending Difficulties and Perplexities — 123
   James Allen
7. Will You Master Money? Or Will It Master You? — 131
   Napoleon Hill
8. The Master Mind — 150
   Napoleon Hill
9. The Realization of Prosperity — 176
   James Allen
10. The Two Masters, Self and Truth — 180
    James Allen

1

VISIONS AND IDEALS

James Allen

The visionaries, the dreamers, hold a sacred role as the guardians and saviors of our world's essence. Just as the tangible world finds its sustenance in the intangible, so too do individuals, amidst their trials, transgressions, and mundane pursuits, draw nourishment from the enchanting visions harbored by these solitary dreamers. Humanity's existence thrives on these dreamers; it clings to their ideals, unwilling to let them dissipate into oblivion. These ideals resonate within humanity, recognized as the very realities that will one day manifest and be embraced.

Consider the artisans of the after-world—the composers, sculptors, painters, poets, prophets, and sages. They stand as the craftsmen of a celestial realm, the creators of a heavenly expanse. Their existence has rendered the world profoundly beautiful; without their presence, the toiling masses of humanity would languish in desolation.

The one who nurtures a sublime vision, an exalted ideal within their soul, possesses the potential to see it materialize. Reflect on Columbus, whose vision of an uncharted world materialized into discovery; Copernicus, who envisioned a universe beyond comprehension, and unfolded its secrets; or Buddha, who glimpsed a spiritual realm of unrivaled purity and tranquility, eventually transcending into its embrace.

These visionary souls set the precedent: the nurturing of a noble vision within one's heart serves as the precursor to its eventual realization. Their stories illuminate the path for others, showcasing the transformative power of envisaging grand ideals—a testament to the potential inherent within every dreaming soul to sculpt their envisioned realities into existence.

Embrace and nurture your visions and ideals, for within them resides the symphony that resonates in your soul—the enchanting melodies, the captivating beauty, the exquisite elegance that adorns your purest thoughts. From these cherished realms sprout the seeds of delightful conditions, shaping the heavenly environment you yearn for. Should you steadfastly hold onto these ideals, they shall eventually sculpt the world you inhabit.

To yearn is to acquire; to aspire is to attain. Should the most basic desires of humanity flourish abundantly while its noblest aspirations languish in deprivation? This imbalance contradicts the natural order; such a discordant state cannot persist—the Law of the universe abides by the principle of "ask and receive."

Envision lofty aspirations, for as you behold these aspirations, so shall you metamorphose. Your Vision serves as a prophecy, foretelling the person you will eventually evolve into; your Ideal is a harbinger of the unveiling of your ultimate self.

Every grand achievement initially existed as a dream. The mighty oak lay dormant within the acorn; the bird awaited its moment within the egg; and within the loftiest vision of the soul, an awakening angel stirs. Dreams, the nascent sparks of reality, carry within them the potential to sprout into tangible manifestations.

BECOMING YOUR VISION

Within the fabric of our circumstances, the potential for transformation lies dormant, awaiting the spark of an Ideal. Consider the tale of a youth ensnared in the grip of adversity: poverty and toil confine him in an unhealthy environment, devoid of refinement and education. Yet, amidst the harshness of his reality, a fervent dream ignites within him—a vision of intelligence, refinement, and beauty. His mind becomes a canvas upon which he paints an ideal existence, embracing wider liberties and boundless opportunities. Driven by an inner unrest, he channels his meager resources and spare moments into nurturing his latent abilities.

Consider the tale of a young soul, entangled in the harsh embrace of poverty and toil, confined within the dismal walls of an unhealthy workplace. Unlettered and devoid of refinement, this youth, against the backdrop of his bleak reality, dares to dream of loftier dimensions. Envisioning intelligence, refinement, grace, and beauty, he meticulously constructs an ideal existence within his mind—a vision of liberation and broader horizons. Stirred by an unrelenting restlessness, he channels every spare moment and scarce resource into the cultivation of his dormant abilities and latent potentials.

With time, a remarkable transformation unfolds within him, rendering the workshop an incongruous setting for his burgeoning mentality. Shedding the workshop like a discarded garment, he emerges, guided by newfound opportunities that align with the expanding scope of his capabilities. Years pass, and the once-youthful dreamer emerges as a mature figure, now a master of formidable mental faculties. His influence reverberates across the globe, his words catalyzing profound changes in the lives of multitudes. A radiant beacon, he becomes the pivot around which numerous destinies orbit, embodying the realization of the vision born during his youth—he has become one with his Ideal.

This narrative underscores the pivotal role of an envisioned Ideal in reshaping destinies. It narrates the tale of a once-constrained dreamer who, through unwavering dedication and relentless pursuit, transcends limitations, metamorphosing into an influential force—an embodiment of the very aspirations that once seemed unattainable.

The tale stands as a testament to the transformative power of an unwavering Ideal, showcasing how a resolute vision, when passionately pursued, becomes the magnetic force propelling an individual toward the realization of their utmost capabilities.

Youthful soul, take heed, for within you lies the potential to actualize the profound Vision that resides in the sanctum of your heart. It matters not whether that Vision appears base, beautiful, or an amalgamation of both; your innate inclination will invariably guide you toward that which you, in the recesses of your being, ardently cherish. The outcomes you receive shall be an exact reflection of your thoughts—an equitable manifestation of your earned merits, no more, no less. Your current surroundings hold no dominion over your fate; rather, it is your thoughts, your Vision, and your Ideal that shall dictate your trajectory—whether you descend, linger, or ascend.

Contemplate the words of Stanton Kirkham Davis—a poetic reflection that encapsulates this truth. Picture yourself meticulously tending to your accounts, ensconced behind a door that once seemed an insurmountable barrier to your aspirations. Then, in a breathtaking moment, you find yourself standing before an audience, your pen poised behind your ear, ink stains marking your fingers, as an inexorable torrent of inspiration surges forth. Or envision yourself amidst the pastoral serenity, tending to sheep, only to wander, wide-eyed and openmouthed, into the city's bustling streets, guided by an intrepid spirit. There, under the tutelage of a master, time transforms you from a mere dreamer into an adept, until the master proclaims, "I have nothing more to teach you." Witness the metamorphosis as you set aside the tools of your trade, assuming the mantle of world regeneration.

These narratives, vivid and stirring, foretell the immutable truth—that your aspirations, your desires, hold the power to shape your reality. You shall scale the heights or descend to the depths in direct proportion to the magnitude of your dominant aspirations and controlling desires. Such is the transformative power wielded by your thoughts, your Vision—a power capable of molding a sheepherder's dreams into a world-altering force.

Consider the perspective of those who lack insight—the thoughtless, the ignorant, and the indolent—who perceive only the superficial outcomes of events without understanding the underlying essence. To them, the success of an individual appears as mere luck or fortune. Witnessing someone amass wealth, they attribute it solely to luck. When observing another attain intellectual prowess, they dub it as sheer favoritism. And upon encountering a saintly figure of wide influence, they hastily attribute it to random chance, neglecting the depth of understanding behind these achievements.

What they fail to discern are the countless trials, failures, and struggles that these individuals willingly confront in their quest for experience. They remain oblivious to the sacrifices made, the relentless efforts exerted, and the unwavering faith embraced to surmount seemingly insurmountable obstacles—all in pursuit of realizing the Vision nestled within their hearts. The onlookers are blind to the darkness and heartaches endured; they only witness the luminosity and exuberance, and dismiss it as "luck."

Their gaze bypasses the extensive and arduous journey, fixating solely on the alluring endpoint, deeming it as mere "good fortune." They are unable to comprehend the intricate process but are quick to label the outcome as "chance."

Thus, their perception remains surface-level, failing to grasp the depth and intricacies of the transformative journey undertaken by these individuals. They misconstrue the profound sacrifices, enduring commitment, and unyielding perseverance as mere strokes of luck or chance, unaware of the profound processes that transpire behind the scenes to manifest these achievements.

There exists an intrinsic correlation between effort and outcome. The potency of the exertion invested invariably determines the magnitude of the result obtained. It is not chance or arbitrary luck that dictates the course of events; rather, it is the unwavering commitment to effort that yields the fruits—be it in the form of gifts, abilities, material possessions, intellectual prowess, or spiritual enlightenment. Each of these stands as a tangible manifestation of completed thoughts, realized visions, and achieved objectives, all rooted in relentless effort and unwavering determination.

The Vision that takes root and flourishes within the chambers of your mind, the Ideal that reigns supreme in the sanctum of your heart—these aren't fleeting sentiments but guiding principles that shape the very fabric of your existence. They are the guiding beacons that steer your life's course, molding your character and defining your destiny. Your aspirations, your dreams, and the ideals you hold dear—they are not passive musings but the blueprints upon which your reality is constructed.

Envision your loftiest ideals, nurture them, and let them permeate every facet of your being. Align your thoughts, actions, and aspirations with these ideals, for they shall serve as the compass that directs your life's voyage. Every stride, every endeavor, guided by these lofty ideals, becomes a stepping stone toward actualizing the life you envision, the person you aspire to be.

Hence, it is through the unwavering pursuit of these cherished ideals—fostered in your mind and enthroned in your heart—that your existence finds its purpose, your journey finds its direction, and your life emerges as a testament to the realization of your innermost aspirations.

2

HOW ATTITUDE AFFECTS RESULTS

Roger Fritz

"I am not saying a Positive Attitude can make you successful. I am saying a Positive Attitude will make you successful."

—Norman Vincent Peale

Understanding the pivotal role of a supervisor in shaping one's job satisfaction and professional growth is undeniably crucial. Whether graced with an inspiring leader, a guiding mentor, or facing challenges with an incompatible boss, an individual's perception and response to their superior profoundly impact their work experience and career trajectory.

The ability to tailor one's approach, molding it to harmonize with the boss's objectives, work style, and preferences, holds immense potential in optimizing the work dynamic. Linda's firsthand encounter within the Purchasing Department serves as a vivid testament to this principle. Recognizing her supervisor Carol's inclination toward meticulousness and a structured work environment, Linda embarked on a deliberate journey of adaptation. She keenly observed Carol's emphasis on punctuality and organization—qualities that markedly contrasted with her previous boss's approach. Driven by a firm resolve to adapt,

Linda initiated intentional shifts in her work habits. She adjusted her schedule, arriving earlier, meticulously organizing her workspace, and even refining her attire to mirror a more conservative demeanor.

This proactive adaptation and alignment with Carol's expectations laid a sturdy foundation for a harmonious and productive relationship. Linda's proactive stance not only fostered a positive work atmosphere but also facilitated her career growth, paving a swift path to advancement within the department.

This anecdote encapsulates the profound impact of adaptability and synchronization with a supervisor's preferences on fostering not just a congenial work environment but also on catalyzing professional advancement and success within an organizational setting.

DO'S AND DON'TS IN DEALING WITH YOUR BOSS

Here are foundational guidelines that can aid in crafting effective coping mechanisms for handling interactions with your supervisor:

The Dos

1. **Observe and Learn from Successful Relationships:**
   - Study colleagues who maintain positive connections with your boss.
   - Note their communication styles, problem-solving approaches, and methods for aligning with the supervisor's expectations.
   - Emulate and adapt their successful strategies to fit your own working style.

2. **Recognize Shared Responsibility:**
   - Acknowledge the potential role your actions might play in a strained relationship.
   - Take ownership of your contributions to the dynamic, focusing on what you can control: your behavior and approach.
3. **Proactive Task Handling:**
   - Offer to manage tasks that your supervisor might not prefer or find time-consuming.
   - Show flexibility and initiative, aiming to ease their workload and reduce potential sources of tension.
4. **Sensitivity to Supervisor's Patterns:**
   - Stay attuned to your boss's mood swings and more approachable times.
   - Use this awareness to time interactions effectively, optimizing the chances for productive engagement.
5. **Thoughtful Expression of Concerns:**
   - Choose the right moment to express your sentiments about your boss's treatment.
   - Wait for a calm and private moment conducive to a constructive conversation.
   - Share your feelings calmly, respectfully, and with a focus on improving the situation.
6. **Monitor, Evaluate, and Adapt:**
   - Continuously monitor your progress in repairing the relationship.
   - If results aren't evident, reevaluate your approach.
   - Adjust your strategy as needed, understanding that meaningful changes take time to manifest in professional relationships. Be patient and persistent in your efforts.

These detailed points encompass a range of proactive strategies, from observation and learning to self-reflection, proactive behavior, sensitivity, effective communication, and adaptive perseverance.

The Don'ts

1. **Respect Employer's Authority:**
   - Uphold your employer's authority, especially during disagreements or differing viewpoints.
   - Avoid engaging in disputes that challenge their authority, as it preserves a professional environment.
   - Express dissent respectfully, focusing on constructive dialogue rather than undermining their authority.
2. **Differentiate Between Criticism and Responsibilities:**
   - Differentiate between criticism related to job responsibilities and personal attacks.
   - Understand that constructive feedback focuses on tasks, not personal traits.
   - Maintain professional equilibrium by acknowledging criticism as a means for improvement, separating it from personal offense.
3. **Exhibit Initiative and Autonomy:**
   - Demonstrate autonomy by taking initiative in executing tasks without constant approval-seeking.
   - Execute necessary actions and inform your boss afterward, showcasing your proactive approach while keeping them updated.
4. **Avoid Gossip and Negative Talk:**
   - Refrain from participating in negative discussions or gossip about your boss behind their back.
   - Exhibit loyalty and professionalism by maintaining

a respectful demeanor and avoiding negative conversations about your supervisor.
5. **Adhere to Established Authority:**
   - Respect the established chain of command; avoid bypassing your boss's authority except in urgent or emergency situations.
   - Recognize that bypassing the hierarchy often complicates issues rather than resolving them efficiently.
6. **Prioritize Self-Respect and Professional Dignity:**
   - Prioritize your self-respect in navigating challenging workplace dynamics.
   - If coping strategies prove ineffective and a transfer isn't feasible, consider exploring opportunities for a new job under a different supervisor.
   - Ensuring professional fulfillment and maintaining dignity in your work environment is paramount for long-term career satisfaction.

These expanded points delve deeper into maintaining a professional demeanor, managing disagreements, exhibiting autonomy, fostering a respectful workplace culture, and prioritizing self-respect in challenging professional scenarios.

It's crucial to underscore the significance of forming judgments based not solely on superficial impressions, such as words or intentions expressed, but rather on a comprehensive evaluation encompassing observed evidence and the tangible outcomes of individuals' actions and behaviors.

In our multifaceted social interactions, initial impressions often stem from verbal expressions or perceived intentions. However, these facets represent only a fraction of a person's entirety. It's through a more nuanced lens that we glean valuable insights into someone's character—their essence revealed not merely through promises or intentions, but manifested in the concrete results of their actions and behaviors.

Observing individuals over time allows us to decipher patterns in their conduct, providing a clearer understanding of their true disposition and reliability. It's this meticulous observation of how individuals navigate challenges, honor commitments, and respond to various situations that paints a more accurate picture of their character.

By grounding our assessments in observable evidence—weighing not just what is said but what is actually done—we fortify our judgments with a more comprehensive understanding. This approach transcends the allure of mere promises or articulated intentions, focusing instead on the tangible manifestations of a person's conduct and choices. It's through this holistic examination that we can form more robust and informed judgments about individuals, ensuring a more accurate portrayal of their character and reliability.

IDENTIFY ACCOUNTABLE PEOPLE

When reflecting on the success or failure of a business, the analysis often transcends mere financial evaluations. While financial stability is undeniably a critical factor, it's often not the sole determinant of a company's downfall. Frequently, the underlying cause of failure traces back to the realization that the wrong individuals were placed in pivotal roles within the organization. This recognition underscores the paramount importance of assessing the dynamics within your professional circle—a composite of your boss, colleagues, and employees—to comprehend their profound influence on the trajectory of your success.

Beyond the tangible assets and financial resources, it's the human element that becomes the linchpin in achieving sustainable business objectives. The attitudes, competencies, and motivations exhibited by those comprising your professional network wield significant sway over the efficacy of your collective efforts. As such, a meticulous examination of each individual's role within this network becomes imperative in driving organizational success.

Consider the pivotal role of your boss—a linchpin figure instrumental in steering the work environment and setting the tone for collaboration and productivity. Their leadership style, communication, and strategic vision can fundamentally shape the ethos of the workplace, impacting employee morale and the overall efficiency of operations.

Furthermore, the contributions of colleagues wield substantial influence. They form the fabric of collaborative efforts, contributing to collective synergy, and can either facilitate innovation or pose challenges that impede progress. Their levels of cooperation, expertise, and attitude profoundly impact the dynamics of teamwork and the pursuit of shared goals.

Similarly, employees represent a critical component in the execution of tasks and the attainment of organizational objectives. Their engagement, dedication, and proficiency directly influence the efficiency and effectiveness of day-to-day operations.

Therefore, a comprehensive evaluation of the people dynamics within a business landscape—a nuanced understanding of each individual's role and impact—becomes indispensable in navigating the path to success. It's through this holistic assessment that businesses can leverage the strengths and mitigate the weaknesses present in their human capital, fostering an environment conducive to growth and achievement.

Engaging in a thorough assessment of whether the individuals within your professional sphere align with your overarching vision, offer constructive support, and actively contribute to collective success emerges as a pivotal task. This evaluation doesn't merely gauge their presence within the framework of your goals but probes deeper into their alignment with your broader vision and the extent of their impact on organizational objectives.

The alignment of these individuals with your vision sets the stage for the harmonious pursuit of shared objectives. When their values, motivations, and objectives align with your overarching vision, it lays the groundwork for a cohesive and unified effort toward collective success. Conversely, a misalignment in goals and values may introduce friction, potentially hindering progress and diverting efforts away from the defined path.

Furthermore, the measure of constructive support offered by these individuals plays a pivotal role in driving organizational growth. Constructive support encompasses not only assistance in achieving set objectives but also a supportive environment that nurtures innovation, collaboration, and a shared sense of purpose. Individuals providing constructive support often foster an environment conducive to exploration, learning, and adaptation, catalyzing the organization's resilience and adaptability in the face of challenges.

Equally critical is the active contribution made by these individuals to the collective success. Their ability to actively participate in furthering organizational goals through innovative ideas, diligent execution, and a proactive approach significantly impacts the momentum of progress. Recognizing and leveraging these contributions can fuel the organization's evolution and competitive edge.

Therefore, the careful assessment of whether these individuals empower or impede progress becomes a guiding beacon in making informed decisions. Identifying individuals who actively contribute to a conducive environment for growth and success allows for strategic alignment, ensuring that the collective efforts propel the organization toward its envisioned objectives. Conversely, acknowledging any factors hindering progress prompts strategic considerations for fostering an environment that nurtures growth and maximizes potential.

The Least Valuable People (LVP) Profile

The "Least Valuable People" profile stands as an invaluable tool in discerning behavioral patterns that bear immense weight in predicting both success and potential setbacks among individuals within professional settings. Its efficacy lies in its ability to offer a structured framework for evaluating personal attributes critical for gauging one's potential for professional advancement or, conversely, the likelihood of facing setbacks.

The inherent simplicity of this profile is encapsulated in its binary response system—guilty or not guilty—a format designed for straightforward assessment. This uncomplicated approach significantly streamlines the process of self-reflection and evaluation of others, fostering a clear and concise method for assessment.

Initiating the evaluation process by self-assessment offers a powerful platform for introspection before extending the assessment to others. This introspective phase allows individuals to closely examine their own behaviors, attitudes, and actions, setting the stage for a more objective and insightful evaluation of others.

What truly makes this profiling tool intriguing is its direct correlation between the listed traits and their indicative nature towards either propelling an individual towards success or hindering their progress. Each trait listed serves as a telltale sign, offering a glimpse into the attitudes and behaviors that either pave the way toward success or act as stumbling blocks.

For instance, traits like avoiding problems, shifting blame for failures, or consistently missing deadlines may signify a lack of accountability and initiative. On the flip side, proactive behaviors such as actively seeking clarification, embracing calculated risks, and nurturing talent within oneself and others are often linked to successful individuals within professional spheres.

The "Least Valuable People" profile, with its binary assessment structure and insightful trait indicators, not only aids in individual self-assessment but also serves as a valuable tool for evaluating others. Its capacity to pinpoint behavioral traits that drive success or impede progress offers a guiding compass for personal development and decision-making in professional realms.

Through a comprehensive analysis of these distinctive traits, individuals gain a nuanced understanding of their positioning concerning attitude and work approach. This introspection becomes a pivotal tool, delineating the fine line between behaviors that foster success and those that pave the way for failure. By discerning and cataloging these attributes, individuals embark on a journey of self-enhancement, utilizing this self-awareness as a compass for personal growth. Moreover, armed with this discerning insight, they adeptly navigate professional landscapes, making judicious choices about professional associations and alliances, thereby ensuring informed and strategic decisions in a professional milieu.

Start by rating yourself first.

	Guilty	Not Guilty
1. Constantly sidesteps problems and complaints, hoping someone else will handle them.		
2. Avoids disciplining people.		
3. Blames others when things go wrong.		
4. Allows false statements to go unchallenged.		
5. Doesn't worry about being late for work or meetings.		
6. Postpones completion of projects as long as possible.		
7. Avoids seeking clarification of misunderstandings in order to criticize later.		
8. Never volunteers for an assignment when not absolutely certain of success.		
9. Doesn't worry about deadlines.		

10. Maintains the same sources of information and bases decisions more on opinions than facts.
11. Tries to be as noncommittal as possible.
12. Punishes good people who disagree.
13. Sees delegating as a way of getting rid of unpleasant chores rather than improving and expanding productivity.
14. Keeps busy on current projects and is uncomfortable about future planning.
15. Allows someone else to do recruiting and selection.
16. Tends to criticize others in public, rather than in private.
17. Is insulated from contact with customers.

18. Frequently talks about how much others depend on them. _____ _____
19. Is not concerned about nurturing promotable people. _____ _____
20. Is uncomfortable when depending on others to provide answers. _____ _____
21. Concentrates efforts on favorite tasks rather than highest priorities. _____ _____
22. Rarely compliments others for their good work. _____ _____
23. Downplays the competence of other people. _____ _____
24. Takes as few risks as possible. _____ _____
25. Waits as long as possible before delivering bad news. _____ _____
26. Limits efforts to "on-the-job" hours; rarely takes work home. _____ _____
27. Is not involved in self-improvement programs. _____ _____

28. Joins in conversations about the "good old days" as often as possible
29. Talks a lot about how difficult it is to objectively measure what they do.
30. Hides talented people to further their own career.

The careful examination and interpretation of the "Guilty" verdicts within the context of your or another individual's behavioral tendencies offer profound and enlightening insights into the potential shaping of their professional trajectory. This breakdown presents a comprehensive analysis based on the number of "Guilty" verdicts, serving as a crucial guide to understanding and navigating the diverse landscapes of professional conduct and development.

In the range of 0–4 Guilty verdicts, the revelation of such a minimal count signifies a commendable and laudable level of accountability and responsibility. Individuals encompassed within this spectrum emerge as invaluable assets within any team or organizational framework. Their contributions not only bolster the efficiency but also significantly enhance the collective productivity of the group. Hence, it becomes imperative to not only recognize but also actively foster and nurture their talents and contributions, ensuring their continued alignment with the organizational goals and ethos.

Moving into the range of 5–10 Guilty verdicts, individuals find themselves in a more complex spectrum, showcasing a blend of both positive and potentially concerning behavioral traits. While their display of accountability is evident, there exist nuances and areas warranting attention and cultivation. With adept guidance, mentorship, and the provision of requisite support mechanisms, these individuals harbor the potential to transform and evolve, acquiring the capability to shoulder enhanced responsibilities. Engaging in strategic coaching and mentorship programs becomes instrumental in harnessing their growth and facilitating their development towards a more refined and effective professional stance.

Stepping into the bracket of 11–20 Guilty verdicts, individuals present a landscape that demands astute observation and careful scrutiny. Their behavioral patterns exhibit a level of concern that could potentially impede the organization's efficiency and overall success. Addressing and rectifying these problematic areas should be a priority. Close monitoring, coupled with timely interventions and targeted development initiatives, become pivotal in redirecting their conduct towards a more constructive and aligned path within the organizational framework.

However, when confronted with a count of "Guilty" verdicts surpassing 20, it signals an alarmingly high frequency, indicative of deeply entrenched behavioral issues and attitudes. Such individuals pose substantial and imminent challenges, potentially jeopardizing the organization's stability and functionality. For supervisors, maintaining documented records of their problematic conduct becomes imperative, seeking guidance and intervention from Human Resources to mitigate risks. In the capacity of a coworker, minimizing direct interactions may serve as a prudent strategy. Should the individual hold a supervisory position, maintaining professionalism while exploring avenues for a departmental transfer could prove beneficial for maintaining organizational harmony and efficacy.

Through the astute interpretation and analysis of these results, a wealth of valuable insights unfolds, illuminating the intricate tapestry of individual behaviors and their prospective impact within a professional setting. This profound understanding serves as a guiding beacon, empowering one to navigate the complex terrain of collaborative endeavors, mentorship dynamics, and the strategic implementation of proactive measures aimed at mitigating and rectifying concerning behavioral patterns.

Delving into these findings unveils a treasure trove of nuanced observations, laying bare the intricate interplay between actions, attitudes, and their potential ramifications. Armed with this discerning insight, individuals possess the capability to make judicious and well-informed decisions pertaining to collaborative ventures. It enables the identification of ideal partners whose compatible behaviors align seamlessly, fostering synergy and productivity while avoiding potential clashes that might impede progress.

Moreover, these revelations serve as a compass for strategic mentorship initiatives. By discerning the behavioral nuances encapsulated within the results, one can tailor mentorship programs and interventions that precisely target areas for growth and enhancement. Such tailored guidance facilitates the evolution of individuals, empowering them to overcome limitations and embrace constructive behavioral paradigms conducive to personal and professional development.

Furthermore, the discernment gleaned from these insights facilitates proactive measures. It allows for the timely identification and proactive addressing of concerning behavioral patterns before they escalate into impediments to productivity or harmony within the professional ecosystem. This proactive stance fosters an environment of continuous improvement and growth, mitigating potential risks and ensuring a more harmonious and effective professional landscape.

Hence, by embracing the depth of understanding offered by these results, individuals not only gain insights into behavioral dynamics but also acquire the strategic acumen necessary to steer collaborations, mentorships, and proactive interventions towards a trajectory of enhanced efficiency, productivity, and professional harmony.

GET THE HELP YOU NEED

> *"Keep away from people who try to belittle your ambitions. Small people always do that, but the really great make you feel that you too can become great."*
>
> —Mark Twain

Recognizing and embracing vulnerability concerning the dependence on others' performance emerges as a defining trait among highly successful individuals. This acknowledgment signifies a deep-rooted awareness of the intricate interdependence prevalent within professional spheres. Successful individuals grasp the profound and far-reaching influence that those around them wield over their own trajectories of accomplishment. Whether it pertains to the collective efforts of a team, the collaborative endeavors with colleagues, or the guidance and leadership provided by mentors and superiors, their recognition of this symbiotic relationship underscores their strategic mindset and astute perception.

These individuals consciously curate their professional environments, deliberately surrounding themselves with individuals whose collective strengths complement and augment their own capabilities. This deliberate act of strategic selection serves as a cornerstone in their pursuit of personal and collective growth. By fostering an ecosystem comprising individuals who not only uplift but also align with their vision and goals, they set the stage for a synergistic collaboration, creating an environment ripe for innovation, productivity, and shared success.

Furthermore, their acknowledgment of vulnerability extends beyond a mere recognition of reliance; it embodies a profound wisdom. They understand that this vulnerability does not diminish their own abilities but rather amplifies their potential. This acknowledgment fosters a mindset conducive to continuous improvement and learning, recognizing that the amalgamation of diverse talents and perspectives nurtures an environment ripe for innovation and unparalleled growth.

Hence, for these successful individuals, acknowledging vulnerability in reliance on others' performance becomes a testament to their strategic foresight and astute understanding of the intricacies woven into the fabric of professional success. It's not merely a sign of dependency but a deliberate and calculated move toward fostering a collaborative ecosystem that propels both personal and collective growth to unprecedented heights.

Utilizing the insights from the LVP (Least Valuable People) profile isn't just about identifying problematic situations; it's also a means to recognize the potential of those who exhibit exceptional qualities:

1. **Exceeding Expectations:** Exceptional individuals set themselves apart by not merely meeting but consistently surpassing existing standards. Their pursuit of progress extends beyond mere compliance with benchmarks, driving them to continually innovate and elevate their performance.
2. **Solution-Driven Mentality:** Instead of dwelling on

problems, these individuals adopt a proactive stance, presenting viable solutions to challenges. They view obstacles as collective issues, leveraging a collaborative approach to propose and implement resolutions.
3. **Resilience Amidst Errors:** Rather than attributing blame elsewhere, these individuals display remarkable resilience in the face of mistakes. They acknowledge errors, taking ownership, and actively explore alternative pathways to rectify and learn from their missteps.
4. **Accountability and Resolution:** When confronted with setbacks, they exhibit accountability without resorting to excuses. Their focus lies not on assigning blame but on swiftly resolving issues and deriving lessons for future improvements.
5. **Effective Self-Management:** Through proactive task management, they navigate complex projects adeptly. By setting interim deadlines and avoiding last-minute rushes, they ensure a smooth and systematic workflow.
6. **Embracing Growth Over Perfection:** Rather than succumbing to the pressures of perfectionism, these individuals prioritize growth and improvement. They understand that the pursuit of perfection often hampers progress, opting instead for continuous enhancement.
7. **Foresight and Strategic Planning:** Forward-thinking individuals anticipate challenges and strategically plan ahead. Their proactive approach minimizes surprises, creating a more controlled and prepared environment.
8. **Unwavering Focus on Forward Momentum:** They don't dwell excessively on past successes or failures. Instead, they swiftly pivot from both triumphs and missteps, focusing on present tasks

and future objectives, fostering a culture of continual advancement.
9. **Inquisitive Nature:** Recognizing the significance of clarity, they actively seek information when uncertainty arises. This commitment to seeking clarity minimizes misunderstandings, ensuring accuracy in communication and decision-making.
10. **Proactive Decision-Making:** Successful individuals don't wait for instructions; they actively negotiate agreements and promptly take action aligned with agreed-upon terms. This proactive approach expedites progress and nurtures innovation within their roles.

In essence, leveraging the insights from the LVP profile goes beyond flagging problematic behaviors; it serves as a powerful tool for recognizing and cultivating individuals showcasing these exceptional qualities, fostering a culture of continuous growth, innovation, and collective success within an organization.

In the intricate tapestry of any organization's dynamics, individuals who proactively initiate, deftly negotiate, and generously share their wealth of knowledge emerge as the linchpins of progress and prosperity. These multifaceted qualities—the art of initiation, the finesse of negotiation, and the altruism in teaching—form the bedrock for driving forward momentum, harmonizing conflicting interests, and nurturing an ecosystem ripe for continual evolution and expansion. Their presence within the organizational framework isn't merely advantageous; it's pivotal for steering the collective towards success.

The astute recognition, deliberate recruitment, adept retention, and purposeful collaboration with individuals exhibiting prowess in these domains represent a strategic investment in the organizational trajectory. Their proficiency in instigating proactive actions, adeptly orchestrating agreements, and generously imparting wisdom and knowledge doesn't just benefit them individually; it becomes a catalyst for empowering the entire team. By leveraging their innate abilities, these individuals become catalysts, propelling the organization forward, aligning actions with aspirations, and fortifying the bedrock of a culture steeped in productivity and seamless collaboration.

Unveiling and appreciating these traits goes beyond a mere risk mitigation strategy. It becomes an opportunity to not only circumvent potential impediments but also to foster symbiotic relationships with individuals whose characteristics seamlessly align with success-oriented behaviors. Collaborating with such stalwarts doesn't merely augment individual endeavors; it serves as a catalyst for elevating the collective team performance. Their innate abilities act as a beacon, illuminating the path toward achieving collective objectives while nurturing an environment ripe for innovation, growth, and unyielding success.

WHAT'S WRONG VS. WHO'S WRONG

The depth of responsibility and attitude, particularly in the context of problem-solving and accountability within organizational settings, warrants an in-depth exploration. At the heart of this exploration lies the pivotal distinction between fixating on the 'who' versus the 'what' when faced with challenges or setbacks.

The emphasis on 'who' inadvertently triggers a perpetual quest to pinpoint fault and assign blame whenever issues arise. This perspective cultivates an atmosphere fraught with tension and defensiveness, shrouding the workspace in a cloud of apprehension. In such environments dominated by a blame-centric culture, team members brace themselves for the imminent rounds of accusations or finger-pointing, inhibiting open communication and collaboration.

Conversely, centering the focus on 'what' transpired, shifts the attention to a more solution-oriented perspective. It steers the collective gaze towards comprehending the intricacies of the problem itself. This approach involves a meticulous analysis of the issue, delving into its root causes, and then mobilizing efforts toward viable and constructive solutions. By emphasizing the 'what,' the organizational environment evolves into a space where individuals channel their energies into proactive problem-solving rather than engaging in a blame game. This fosters a collaborative culture, where team members unite their strengths, working in unison to tackle challenges with a shared commitment to finding solutions. It's an environment characterized by open communication, mutual support, and a collective drive toward progress.

The critical differentiation between fixating on 'who' and 'what' encapsulates the core essence of a positive attitude and a culture of accountability within an organization. While the former perpetuates a cycle of tension and defensiveness, the latter cultivates an atmosphere ripe for innovation and collaboration. It's about channeling efforts into understanding and resolving issues collectively, steering away from assigning blame and focusing on constructive problem-solving strategies that ultimately propel the organization toward sustainable success.

Hence, the cultivation of a conducive workplace atmosphere stands as an imperative. It necessitates the nurturing of an environment that steers clear of fixating on attributing blame to individuals but rather rallies around a collective focus on addressing the underlying problems. A culture that not only prioritizes but actively encourages problem-solving and constructive dialogues over the futile pursuit of fault-finding emerges as a cornerstone in organizational dynamics.

Embracing such a culture births an ethos steeped in open communication, transparency, and a shared sense of accountability. It lays the foundation for a collaborative approach, where individuals unite in a common resolve to surmount challenges rather than engaging in a futile blame game. This concerted effort towards solution-oriented discussions propels the organization toward innovative strategies, fostering an environment teeming with growth opportunities and forward-thinking initiatives.

This culture shift doesn't merely serve as a catalyst for innovation and development; it becomes the very fabric that weaves a tapestry of positivity and productivity within the workspace. By placing emphasis on problem-solving rather than on assigning blame, it nurtures an atmosphere where every member feels valued and empowered to contribute to the collective resolution of challenges. This sense of inclusivity and collective responsibility not only drives progress but also significantly shapes a work environment that thrives on positivity, collaboration, and shared success.

The cultivation of a workplace ethos centered on problem-solving transcends mere functionality; it evolves into a guiding philosophy that not only propels innovation and growth but also anchors the organization within the realms of a harmonious, positive, and remarkably productive workspace.

ATTITUDE AND EFFECTIVENESS

"Success or failure in business is caused more by mental attitude than by mental capacities."

—Sir Walter Scott

The correlation between effectiveness in leadership roles and attitude forms a nuanced and often underestimated connection, one that profoundly impacts the trajectory of leadership success. Surprisingly, attitude stands as a fundamental cornerstone, intricately interwoven with the fabric of leadership effectiveness. For supervisors, managers, or leaders navigating the intricate landscapes of their roles, the evaluation of their effectiveness invariably hinges upon the pervasive influence their attitude wields over the outcomes achieved.

In the realm of leadership, engaging in profound self-reflection stands as a pivotal tool, offering a revealing lens through which to assess the impact of one's attitude. This introspective journey involves posing pivotal questions that delve into the essence of how attitudes shape the contours of effective leadership. Questions that scrutinize the depths of personal beliefs, responses to adversity, approaches to decision-making, and interactions with team members serve as guiding beacons in unraveling the intricate tapestry of leadership attitudes.

By engaging in this introspective process, leaders gain profound insights into the alignment between their attitudes and the consequential outcomes within their spheres of influence. It's an exercise that transcends mere evaluation; it becomes a pathway toward self-awareness, fostering an acute understanding of the correlation between attitude and leadership efficacy.

The significance of attitude within leadership roles permeates beyond mere perceptions; it permeates through actions, decisions, and the overall organizational climate. A positive and proactive attitude exerts an indelible influence, not just shaping individual leadership styles but also sculpting team dynamics, organizational culture, and, ultimately, the achievements realized.

Therefore, delving into the undercurrents of one's attitude stands as a transformative journey, a voyage that not only augments leadership effectiveness but also serves as a catalyst for personal growth and the cultivation of a dynamic, impactful leadership ethos within the broader organizational landscape.

To comprehensively gauge the profound impact of your attitude on the success of the team under your leadership, a meticulous examination through these fundamental inquiries becomes imperative:

1. **Demonstrating Genuine Support:** An introspective evaluation should seek factual evidence showcasing your authentic dedication to the success and growth of those under your guidance. Your attitude should resonate with a genuine desire to nurture and uplift team members towards collective success.
2. **Commitment to Planning and Resourcing:** Assess whether your behavior reflects an unwavering commitment to investing adequate time in strategic planning, foreseeing future needs, and diligently providing essential resources essential for your team's effectiveness and growth.
3. **Composure Amidst Crises:** The evaluation extends to your demeanor during crises or emergencies. Can you maintain a composed stance, steering clear of impulsive reactions that might adversely impact your team's response? Your ability to maintain calmness becomes

instrumental in guiding the team through challenging situations.

4. **Fostering a Risk-Tolerant Environment:** Delve into whether you nurture an environment conducive to calculated risk-taking. Evaluate if you refrain from penalizing messengers of unfavorable news, fostering a culture where divergent views are embraced without repercussions.

5. **Handling Disagreements with Diplomacy:** Assess your aptitude in managing disagreements, ensuring they don't escalate into discord. Your approach towards resolving conflicts speaks volumes about your attitude towards fostering healthy interactions within the team.

6. **Mitigating Power Imbalances:** Evaluate if you actively avoid showcasing symbols of status or privilege that might inadvertently induce fear, isolation, or suspicion among team members. Cultivating an environment of equality and inclusivity rests on mitigating perceived power imbalances.

7. **Guiding and Coaching:** Scrutinize your skills in negotiating challenging yet attainable goals. Can you adeptly guide rather than dictate, coach instead of command, ensuring a collaborative approach to goal setting and achievement?

8. **Information Readiness:** Reflect on your readiness to swiftly acquire necessary information. While omniscience isn't expected, minimizing surprises and possessing the ability to access pertinent information swiftly stand as crucial aspects of leadership preparedness.

9. **Clarity in Communication:** Evaluate your aptitude in simplifying complex issues and ensuring

communications are easily comprehensible. Reducing instances requiring clarification facilitates smoother operations and clearer directives for the team.
10. **Embracing Diverse Opinions:** Assess your approach to encouraging dissenting opinions. Acknowledge that unanimity might not always equate to thorough examination. Creating an environment where differing perspectives are valued contributes to comprehensive decision-making, reminiscent of the practice of Alfred Sloan.

These inquiries offer a comprehensive lens to scrutinize the impact of your attitude on the team's success. They serve as guiding principles to align leadership behaviors and attitudes with the collective success and growth of the team.

Engaging with and proactively addressing these probing inquiries stands as a cornerstone in sculpting and refining your prowess as a leader. The proactive endeavor to not only address but earnestly adjust attitudes and behaviors based on the insightful responses gleaned from these evaluations holds the potential to significantly mold and enhance your effectiveness at the helm of leadership.

The pivotal significance lies in the willingness to embark on an introspective journey, exploring the depths of one's attitudes, and embracing adaptive measures where necessary. This transformative process sets the stage for fostering an environment conducive to continual growth, fostering an ecosystem ripe for innovation, and ultimately paving the path toward a tapestry woven with the threads of success within the team or broader organizational landscape.

Conversely, an inability to offer coherent and substantial answers to these pivotal inquiries unveils a chasm in self-awareness. This lack of clarity not only signals a void in comprehending one's attitudes but might also cast shadows on the transparency regarding how these attitudes manifest and impact the organizational ecosystem. Decision-makers vested with assessing your potential for career progression often rely on tangible evidence encapsulating how your attitudes manifest and shape your contributions within the organizational context.

The crux lies in the alignment between articulated attitudes and manifested behaviors. Your actions serve as tangible reflections, painting a vivid picture of how your attitudes seamlessly intertwine with your engagements—be it with tasks, colleagues, or the myriad challenges encountered within the professional sphere. This coherence between professed attitudes and exhibited behaviors becomes a guiding compass for others, offering insights into your approach, values, and unwavering commitment to steering the organization toward its overarching goals.

Ergo, ensuring an unwavering consistency between professed attitudes and demonstrated actions emerges as an instrumental facet in crafting a compelling narrative for career advancement. It becomes a narrative woven intricately with the threads of credibility, authenticity, and a resolute commitment to embodying attitudes that not only espouse but actively drive the organization's vision and aspirations forward.

OVERCOMING YOUR OWN NEGATIVE ATTITUDES

"The greatest discovery of my generation is that a human being can alter their life by altering attitudes."

—William James

Encountering the realization that one's actions or attitudes contribute to an issue signifies an invaluable opportunity for personal growth and development. In these pivotal moments of self-realization, employing strategic strategies can profoundly shape one's responses and foster a pathway towards positive transformation:

1. **Reflecting on Negative Attitudes:** Devoting a moment to scrutinize negative attitudes allows individuals to forecast their potential implications. By questioning the trajectory of these attitudes, individuals gain a profound sense of clarity about the detrimental consequences of persisting with such mindsets.
2. **Embracing Humor as an Antidote:** Laughter stands as a powerful antidote to adversities. Its remarkable ability to alleviate stress and infuse levity into challenging situations makes humor an effective coping mechanism, aiding in navigating difficult moments.
3. **Maintaining a Positive Outlook in Setbacks:** Acknowledging setbacks as an inherent facet of life, while simultaneously maintaining a positive perspective, serves as a potent strategy to mitigate the duration and severity of problems. This resilience in the face of adversity aids in recalibrating attitudes towards a more constructive outlook.
4. **Harnessing the Power of Self-Talk:** Engaging in calming self-talk during stressful times significantly reduces stress levels. Moments taken for breaks, such as stepping away for lunch or short breaks, offer valuable opportunities to unwind and recharge.
5. **Cultivating Positive Self-Talk:** When faced with moments of low spirits, fostering positive affirmations

within oneself serves as an uplifting mechanism, enhancing mood and shifting outlook towards a more optimistic horizon.
6. **Realigning Priorities and Goals:** Assessing whether personal aspirations align with genuine desires or are shaped by external expectations becomes crucial. Authenticity in goal-setting serves as a linchpin for personal contentment and fulfillment.
7. **Simplifying Complexity:** Streamlining complexities wherever possible aids in efficient decision-making and minimizes unnecessary stress. Simplification serves as a compass, guiding individuals towards clarity and ease in handling challenges.
8. **Preventing Escalation of Minor Issues:** Nipping minor problems in the bud prevents their escalation into larger, more formidable issues. Addressing these issues early on minimizes their potential to snowball into more significant challenges.
9. **Nurturing Meaningful Connections:** Investing in nurturing relationships with family and friends enriches life experiences. Maintaining these connections becomes a buffer during trying times, requiring equal dedication as that dedicated to professional roles.
10. **Embracing Collaborative Problem-Solving:** Engaging in brainstorming sessions to generate positive solutions with others fosters a constructive approach. Reflecting on alternative actions or words that could have yielded a more positive outcome becomes a valuable exercise in growth and learning from shared experiences.

In essence, the strategic deployment of these approaches during moments of self-realization steers individuals towards a path of self-improvement and resilience. These strategies serve as catalysts for personal growth, fostering a mindset poised for adaptation, learning, and continual enhancement.

Embarking upon the transformative journey of change and growth intricately weaves a narrative fraught with formidable challenges. It's a narrative that unfolds through acts demanding immense courage, humility, and unwavering resilience. The acts of apologizing for past missteps, initiating a fresh start, humbly acknowledging one's mistakes, persistently striving for improvement, and heeding advice seldom manifest effortlessly. These endeavors demand a profound willingness to confront not just one's own shortcomings but also the skepticism or even disdain from those around us.

Navigating the intricate terrain of avoiding errors proves to be an arduous task, as some missteps often seem inevitable despite our earnest intentions. The pursuit of sustained success brings its own labyrinth of complexities; the alluring diversions that beckon incessantly test our resolve, making it immensely challenging to remain resolute on the unwavering path to achievement.

Breaking free from detrimental habits demands considerable effort, requiring a deliberate departure from monotonous routines and embracing the liberating power of forgiveness. It's a journey that necessitates exercising caution in our actions, taming the tempestuous nature within us, and bravely shouldering the weight of deserved blame when necessary. These endeavors are not for the faint-hearted; they demand an unwavering commitment and inner fortitude.

Undoubtedly, these undertakings stand as formidable challenges, yet they also serve as the very stepping stones that pave the way to brighter tomorrows. They guide us through a transformative realm of personal growth, leading us towards a realm of greater fulfillment and, ultimately, a more enriched existence. The rewards that stem from this journey towards change and growth far outweigh the trials encountered along the way. They form the bedrock of an evolving narrative, one that propels us towards a life brimming with resilience, wisdom, and the boundless potential of continual growth.

BUILD UP YOUR SELF-CONFIDENCE

"If you have a positive attitude and constantly strive to give your best effort, eventually you will overcome your immediate problems and find you are ready for greater challenges."

— Pat Riley

The journey of learning to believe in oneself stands as a fundamental pillar in the construction of confidence, a quality that threads through the tapestry of every facet of our lives. At its core, our attitude functions as a multifaceted mirror, reflecting the myriad facets of our personality, prominently showcasing the degree of confidence we hold within.

The pursuit of bolstering self-assurance necessitates a concerted effort towards addressing pivotal aspects integral to this journey. Firstly, acknowledging one's limitations serves as a foundational cornerstone for personal growth. Embracing and understanding these limitations becomes not a hindrance but a catalyst for self-improvement and evolution. By recognizing these areas for development, individuals create fertile ground for fostering resilience and adaptability, key components of a confident demeanor.

Secondly, honing the skill of effective decision-making contributes significantly to nurturing self-confidence. The ability to make informed choices, rooted in self-awareness and clarity, shapes an individual's belief in their own capabilities. Expanding awareness and sharpening these crucial components fosters a robust framework, providing scaffolding for the construction and nurturing of belief in oneself.

Moreover, this journey towards self-belief and confidence isn't merely a destination; it's a continual process of introspection, growth, and refinement. Embracing and overcoming limitations, coupled with honing decision-making skills, sets the stage for an unwavering belief in oneself. It cultivates an inner landscape that exudes assurance, resilience, and an unyielding spirit in the face of challenges.

The process of building self-belief and confidence is transformative, empowering individuals to navigate life's complexities with an unwavering sense of self-assuredness. As this inner belief expands, it permeates every facet of our interactions, professional endeavors, and personal aspirations, ultimately shaping a life brimming with assurance, purpose, and the unbounded potential of self-belief.

What Limitations Will You Accept?

Jimmy Heuga's story in the skiing world during the 1960s was nothing short of remarkable. His prowess was undeniable, evidenced by his clinching of a bronze medal in the 1964 Olympic slalom. However, the tide turned when, at twenty-five, his disappointment was palpable as he landed an eighth-place finish in the same event in 1968. What seemed like a moment of athletic decline concealed a profound struggle unbeknownst to many—he was battling the onset of multiple sclerosis, a diagnosis that came as a staggering blow.

The grim prognoses delivered by several doctors painted

a bleak picture, deeming his nerve damage severe enough to potentially confine him to a wheelchair. Yet, Heuga staunchly rejected this fate. Instead, he embarked on an extraordinary journey, one defined by an unwavering determination to defy the limitations imposed by his condition. In the face of what seemed insurmountable, he refused to succumb to helplessness.

Embracing an unyielding spirit, Heuga adopted an intense and disciplined routine, commuting on his bicycle, engaging in rigorous daily exercise, and dedicating twenty minutes to swimming—a testament to his resilience and sheer determination. Moreover, he embarked on the daunting task of relearning how to ski, defying the odds and pushing through the hurdles posed by his illness.

His story is a testament to the power of human resilience, an ode to the indomitable spirit that refuses to yield even in the face of seemingly insurmountable challenges. Heuga's unwavering resolve to push beyond the confines of his diagnosis serves as an inspiring narrative—a testament to the human spirit's capacity to defy the limitations imposed by circumstances. His legacy extends far beyond the ski slopes, encapsulating a profound message of perseverance and the unwavering belief in the human potential to triumph over adversity.

At the core of Jimmy Heuga's ethos lay a resolute conviction—a belief that while he could have resigned himself to the confinement of a wheelchair, the prospect of idleness and dependence was inconceivable. His unwavering vision centered on revitalizing his life through the cultivation of a robust health regimen, one that transcended the limitations imposed by his diagnosis.

His straightforward philosophy, deeply ingrained in resilience, resonates profoundly: navigate around the obstacles posed by the disease. Heuga likened this approach to the incremental steps taken in learning to swim—an analogy where initial hesitations are overcome by merely dipping one's feet into the water, gradually wading deeper each day until confidence in swimming is attained.

This mindset became the bedrock not only for Heuga's personal journey in confronting and managing his illness but also served as the catalyst that galvanized him to establish the Heuga Center. This foundation stands as a testament to his unwavering commitment, offering tailored programs borne from his own experiences to assist others in their battles against MS. The center stands tall as a beacon of hope and resilience, illuminating the path for countless individuals traversing the challenging terrain of multiple sclerosis.

Indeed, Jimmy Heuga's story isn't merely one of personal triumph; it embodies a profound lesson—an invaluable narrative underscoring the importance of resilience, perseverance, and the unwavering ability to adapt in the face of adversity. His legacy extends far beyond individual accomplishments, casting ripples of inspiration that resonate across barriers and serve as guiding principles for those navigating their own trials and tribulations. Heuga's indomitable spirit and approach offer a timeless beacon of guidance—a testament to the extraordinary strength that lies within the human spirit to triumph over adversity and transform challenges into opportunities for growth and resilience.

What Choices Do You Make?

Ann Weber, a distinguished psychologist hailing from Asheville, North Carolina, brings to light the inherent discomfort entwined with the act of decision-making, attributing it to the weighty burden of responsibility that choices carry. She astutely observes the allure of indecision, a seemingly safe refuge where the burden of blame finds no purchase. However, Weber eloquently emphasizes the perilous downside of this refuge: a life spiraling beyond one's control, ensnared in the stagnancy bred by perpetual indecision.

Delving deeper into the labyrinth of indecision, Jane Burka, a respected psychologist based in Berkeley, California, meticulously delineates the array of personality archetypes grappling with the complexities of decisiveness. Her insights illuminate various personas navigating the daunting landscape of decision-making. The perfectionists, wary of errors and the consequences thereof, opt to evade decisions rather than risk any potential misstep. On the other hand, non-compromisers adamantly strive for the unattainable, feeling compromised at the mere hint of relinquishment. Then there are the freedom lovers, confronted with a myriad of choices, who instinctively balk at commitments, perpetually seeking open-ended options. Lastly, the dependents, inclined to place greater trust in others' judgments than in their own, navigate life through the lens of external validation.

What intricately ties together these disparate personas, as astutely pointed out, is a common thread of lacking self-esteem, intricately woven into the fabric of their upbringing. The roots of the perfectionist's reluctance might stem from a familial environment where errors were met with harsh criticism, cultivating a fear of imperfection. Dependents, too, might have been conditioned by constant admonitions regarding their decision-making abilities, fostering a sense of resignation in their own judgments due to a lack of nurtured confidence.

The profound insights offered by Weber and Burka serve as illuminating signposts, unveiling the intricate connections between indecision and the bedrock of self-esteem. Their observations highlight the often-overlooked yet profound impact of upbringing and past experiences on shaping an individual's approach to decision-making and self-assurance. Understanding these nuanced connections becomes a pivotal step towards fostering a more confident and decisive outlook, steering individuals away from the paralyzing grasp of perpetual indecision and towards a path of empowered choices and self-assuredness.

Mike Hernacki, a writer from San Diego, echoes this sentiment, attributing his own lack of self-assurance and ensuing indecisiveness to his unforgiving upbringing. His childhood was steeped in a puritanical ethos, an environment where praise was a rarity, and any achievement fell short of absolute perfection. He reminisces about receiving stellar grades, only to be met with a dismissive "What's with the B?" from his father.

In reflecting on pivotal moments in their lives, both Hernacki and Frank McCourt illuminate the intricate journey towards fulfilling their aspirations against formidable odds.

Hernacki's life journey traversed various career trajectories, from teaching to advertising, law, and stockbroking. Despite dating the same woman for four years, he found himself unable to summon the courage to propose until she issued a decisive ultimatum. However, despite these life changes and endeavors, his ultimate aspiration to become a writer remained dormant for a staggering fourteen years. He harbored a fixation on monetary gain, convinced that his prior professions failed to yield substantial income, inadvertently relegating his passion for writing to the back burner.

Similarly, Frank McCourt's odyssey from Ireland to the United States was fraught with daunting adversity. Arriving in America penniless, lacking in skills, and devoid of companionship, he found himself embroiled in menial and grueling jobs, toiling tirelessly to finance his college education.

Despite harboring aspirations to write, McCourt found himself navigating a path as a teacher of English in New York City high schools. However, it wasn't until retirement that he unearthed the self-assurance and inner conviction to pursue his long-held aspirations in writing.

It's the tales of these two individuals, Hernacki and McCourt, that underscore the profound realization that the pursuit of one's passions often faces unforeseen hurdles. Hernacki's fixation on financial stability veiled his inherent passion for writing for an extensive period, while McCourt's journey was marked by a life of toil and teaching before seizing the opportunity to pursue his writing aspirations.

However, both narratives beautifully epitomize the indomitable human spirit and the undeterred pursuit of aspirations against the backdrop of adversity. Hernacki's belated but pivotal realization and McCourt's eventual triumph with the publication of "Angela's Ashes" serve as powerful reminders that the journey towards realizing one's aspirations often requires resilience, perseverance, and an unwavering commitment to follow one's passion, even in the face of seemingly insurmountable odds. Their journeys stand as beacons of inspiration, echoing the timeless lesson that the pursuit of one's dreams is a path often carved amidst challenges, yet it remains an undeniable testament to the resilience of the human spirit.

In their transformative book, "The Confidence Quotient: 10 Steps to Conquer Self-Doubt," psychologists Meryle Gillman and Diane Gage delve into the intricate psyche of the indecisive, offering insightful counsel aimed at empowering individuals to conquer the grip of self-doubt. Their approach advocates for a critical recognition of the negative influences that have shaped an individual's outlook, inviting them to embark on a visualization exercise as a means of introspection and transformation.

Gillman and Gage's exercise is a powerful tool—a mental canvas where individuals identify the doubters in their lives, be it a critical parent, a discouraging mentor, or any negative influence, juxtaposed with a reinforcement figure—a beacon of consistent support and encouragement. This exercise seeks to reframe the internal dialogue, fostering a symbiotic relationship between doubt and encouragement. By visualizing these contrasting figures, individuals recalibrate their mental landscape, cultivating a positive alliance between doubt and reinforcement. This transformative process significantly influences the approach to decision-making, showcasing that regardless of the outcome, the world doesn't crumble—an empowering realization that bolsters one's sense of control over their choices and their lives.

These anecdotes collectively underscore the profound impact of early upbringing on an individual's confidence and decisiveness. They highlight the pivotal role played by childhood environments in sculpting an individual's self-perception and approach towards decision-making. The significance of fostering an environment that nurtures self-esteem and cultivates the courage to make choices free from fear of judgment or reproach becomes abundantly clear through these insights.

Moreover, the journey toward becoming more decisive isn't a leap but a series of purposeful steps taken daily. Waiting for an elusive sense of absolute control before making choices is akin to postponing quitting smoking until the taste becomes unpleasant—an elusive scenario. Instead, Gillman and Gage advocate for initiating a series of small decisions as the foundational groundwork for fostering decisiveness. It's about setting a course of action, making intentional choices, and committing to them—a process akin to saying, "I'll take steps to quit smoking," and then diligently following through on that commitment. These incremental decisions form the bedrock for nurturing decisiveness, empowering individuals to navigate life's myriad choices with confidence, clarity, and an unwavering sense of self-assurance.

Indecisiveness often roots itself in the apprehension surrounding an unknown future—a daunting landscape rife with uncertainties. Yet, an intriguing phenomenon unfolds upon taking action: the perceived horror of these uncertainties tends to diminish. The strategy, as many experts propose, revolves around dissecting decisions into manageable, bite-sized steps. Consider navigating the realm of personal investments, for instance. Instead of delving into the vast expanse of the entire stock market, the focus shifts to acquiring essential knowledge about specific investments—an approach that's smaller, more digestible, and less overwhelming.

This perspective echoes the wisdom of Mike Hernacki, whose profound insights resonate deeply in this context. Hernacki posits that the significance of decisions lies not solely in their immediate impact but predominantly in the commitment behind them. Moreover, he advocates that contrary to popular belief, the majority of decisions aren't as pivotal as one might imagine, and very few hold the potential to be truly fatal. What truly matters, he contends, is the dedication to making these decisions work, irrespective of their magnitude.

Reflecting on his own journey, Hernacki candidly acknowledges that decision-making hasn't always come effortlessly, even in the present. However, the evolution in his approach is remarkable. He emphasizes the transformative power inherent in accumulating a history of decisions—a repository of experiences that collectively bolster confidence and actively shape one's approach to decision-making. This metamorphosis signifies a profound shift in mindset—from hesitancy and reservation to an assertive attitude of "getting out there and making them."

The journey toward becoming more decisive, as illustrated by Hernacki's insights, is a continuous evolution—a progression from apprehension to confidence, fostered by a cumulative wealth of decision-making experiences. It's about understanding that amidst the uncertainties of life, the power lies in embracing decisions—whether big or small—with commitment and resolve. Each decision becomes a stepping stone, not just toward a particular outcome, but toward the cultivation of a confident and assertive approach that navigates the twists and turns of life's uncertainties with unwavering determination.

In essence, this approach encapsulates the fundamental significance of adopting a proactive stance in decision-making. It transcends the mere magnitude of decisions, emphasizing instead the pivotal role of commitment in seeing them through. It's about understanding that the potency of decisions doesn't solely reside in their immediate impact, but rather in the dedication and persistence applied to their execution.

This perspective unveils a transformative truth: taking consistent, incremental steps lays the groundwork for fostering a more decisive and empowered approach to life's myriad choices. It's the culmination of these smaller, purposeful actions that construct the foundation for navigating future decisions with a sense of assurance and confidence. Each deliberate step forward contributes to the cultivation of a mindset—one rooted in proactivity and resolve—that reshapes the narrative of decision-making from one of uncertainty to one of empowerment.

Embracing this proactive approach isn't just about the decisions themselves; it's about the evolution of our mindset—a shift from passive contemplation to active engagement. It's an acknowledgment that by consistently taking steps, regardless of their size, we pave the way toward a future characterized by decisiveness, self-assurance, and an unwavering commitment to charting our own path. Ultimately, this proactive stance transcends the scope of individual decisions, becoming a guiding principle that infuses our lives with resilience, empowerment, and the conviction to navigate the complexities of choice with unwavering determination.

"Positive attitude enables us to focus not on uncontrollable events or circumstances, but on our response to them."

3

SELF-CONTROL

Napoleon Hill

Self-control operates as a silent architect shaping the intricate structure of our actions, serving as the sturdy axis upon which the trajectory of our choices pivots. It stands as the linchpin of our emotional equilibrium, fostering constructive outcomes instead of chaotic downfall, intricately weaving a tapestry that defines our lives.

Visualize a finely tuned instrument where enthusiasm and self-control harmoniously dance, each contributing its unique melody to the symphony of life. The staggering revelation that a striking ninety-two percent of incarcerated individuals lack this pivotal attribute shines a glaring light on its monumental impact in steering the courses of our destinies. This fact, as shocking as it is authentic, underscores the critical role self-control plays in shaping the fabric of our lives.

The absence of self-control becomes a fertile soil for the seeds of regret and misfortune to flourish. Across the corridors of religious texts and philosophical teachings, the resounding call for self-mastery echoes. Even within the depths of scriptures, the exhortation to practice forgiveness and non-resistance stands as a testament to the sanctity of self-control.

Delve into the annals of history, and a common thread weaves through the narratives of the revered—the mastery of self-control. Take Abraham Lincoln, weathering trials that would test the resolve of any leader, yet exuding patience and unwavering poise. His capacity to transcend personal grievances in service of the greater good stands as a timeless testament to the sheer power of self-control.

Yet, pause and consider, how many among us wield the mastery of self-control to such an extent? In the pulpit, fiery words resound about the repugnance of those who seek to belittle others for personal gain. The raw candor of figures like Billy Sunday strikes a chord, unveiling the darker side of those devoid of self-restraint. Even the metaphorical "devil" might nod in agreement at these stark truths, showcasing the profound implications of lacking self-control in the human experience.

Within the discourse on the Law of Success, the concept of self-control transcends its traditional perception as a moral virtue. It emerges as an indispensable tool wielded by those aspiring for accomplishment, transcending the mere realm of ethical conduct. It's not merely the absence of harm inflicted upon others; rather, it stands as the mastery of a potent force requisite for personal advancement—a crucial attribute that separates those on the path to success from the rest.

Failure to exercise self-control not only harbors the risk of causing harm to others but also guarantees self-inflicted wounds. It signifies the voluntary relinquishment of a vital strength, akin to discarding a key tool necessary for navigating the intricate journey toward success. It's the surrender of a guiding compass that steers one's actions towards the attainment of desired objectives.

Self-discipline acts as the linchpin, intricately interconnecting various facets crucial for achievement:

personal drive, an optimistic mindset, and a balanced fervor for progress. It emerges as the pivotal force that intricately intertwines these multifaceted aspects—an amalgamation of concerted efforts culminating in eventual success. Achieving self-discipline necessitates a progressive evolution in these other areas, demanding not only a profound understanding of oneself but also a realistic appraisal of one's current capacities and limitations. In turn, without self-discipline acting as the guiding force, these principles remain dormant—mere seeds waiting for the nurturing influence necessary to manifest into actionable steps towards success.

Envision your mind as an expansive reservoir teeming with untapped potential, awaiting its harnessing. Self-discipline stands as the essential conduit, meticulously guiding this reservoir's energy in measured doses and precise directions. It encapsulates the very essence of self-control, functioning as the artful means by which you channel your personal power toward achieving success with precision and intent.

Central to the realm of self-discipline lies the regulation of emotions—a fundamental aspect that requires mastery. Rather than succumbing to impulsive actions driven by unchecked emotions, self-discipline urges a reversal of this pattern—a deliberate pause for contemplation before reacting. This mastery involves attaining control over your emotions, placing a premium on emotional intelligence and mindfulness. Reflecting on the spectrum of emotions, it becomes evident that unchecked negative emotions possess the potential to wreak havoc if left unbridled. Even seemingly positive emotions, when unorganized and unleashed without conscious regulation, hold the potential for upheaval. There exists within these emotions a formidable force—a volatile potency that, when harnessed adeptly, propels individuals toward great achievements. However, when allowed to roam freely without restraint, they possess the capacity to drive one toward the cliffs of failure.

At the foundation of achievement lies a definitive major purpose, fueled by an unequivocal and compelling motive. This driving force must possess the potency to align your thoughts and endeavors singularly toward the attainment of your goals. However, it's imperative to acknowledge that while emotional vigor serves as the fuel behind your drive, it shouldn't overpower your prudence. Discipline remains paramount in this pursuit. Your enthusiasm and desires must harmonize with control, channeled effectively and judiciously. This harmony between fervor and discipline becomes the cornerstone upon which successful endeavors are built—a delicate equilibrium that steers you toward your aspirations while ensuring a steady course anchored in mindful control.

Self-discipline emerges as a nuanced art of harmonizing the ebbs and flows of emotions with the steadiness of reason. It beckons a careful consultation of both sentiments and logic before delving into the realm of decision-making. At times, the dictates of rationality must assert dominance over emotions, ensuring a clear-headed assessment, while in other instances, decisions might lean towards the sway of emotions, albeit tempered and guided by reason. Striking this balance emerges as a critical juncture in the pursuit of self-discipline—a delicate equilibrium where emotions and reason intersect to pave the way for wise choices and purposeful actions.

Consider the narrative of individuals engulfed in the immersive embrace of all-consuming love. Entrapped within this emotional tempest, they risk losing sight of their own life purposes, becoming easily swayed and manipulated by the intensity of their emotions. Yet, veering solely towards rigid rationality, devoid of the hues of emotions, isn't a panacea either.

Emotions, akin to the flowing currents of a river, possess an inherent energy—a driving force that empowers and propels our actions forward. Attempting to obliterate emotions, such as hope, faith, enthusiasm, or desire, while retaining reason, would render reason directionless and devoid of purpose. Instead, the essence lies in navigating and channeling these emotions, steering their flow rather than attempting their annihilation—an endeavor that would prove futile in the ever-changing landscape of human emotions.

Even the realm of negative emotions, often perceived as turbulent waters, holds the potential to be managed and directed towards constructive ends through the interplay of Positive Mental Attitude (PMA) and self-discipline. Fear or anger, when harnessed and kept under control, can serve as catalysts for prompt and intense action. However, subjecting both negative and positive emotions to scrutiny before their release into the world becomes paramount. Emotions, untethered from the realms of reason, can manifest as formidable adversaries, disrupting the harmony between deliberate action and thoughtful decision-making. It's within the fusion of emotions and reason, delicately balanced and skillfully guided, that the true essence of self-discipline and its transformative potential come to fruition.

The equilibrium between reason and emotion finds its facilitator in the realm of your willpower or ego—an intricate force that navigates the interplay between these fundamental aspects of human existence. In the intricate tapestry of self-discipline, this balancing act gains amplification, allowing you to harness the intensity and direction of their expression. Your ego, functioning as the master conductor, reigns over the symphony of your heart and mind—a sovereign force guiding their harmonious collaboration. However, this mastery is contingent upon the exercise of self-discipline—a deliberate and conscious effort to regulate and steer these forces towards a unified purpose.

When self-discipline is adeptly employed, the ego becomes the harbinger of balance, ensuring that reason and emotion complement rather than collide. It establishes a dynamic equilibrium, preventing the discordant clashes between heart and mind that often leave internal scars—wounds inflicted by the tumultuous battles waged within.

Without the firm hand of self-discipline guiding the ego's mastery, chaos reigns within, and the delicate balance between reason and emotion is jeopardized. In the absence of this disciplined approach, the mind and heart engage in a relentless struggle, each vying for dominance, leaving the individual caught in the crossfire of their internal conflicts—a state of internal disarray that impedes progress and personal growth. Hence, self-discipline emerges as the linchpin, the guiding force that allows the ego to reign supreme, orchestrating the intricate dance between reason and emotion towards a harmonious and purposeful coexistence.

THE BIG FOUR

Self-discipline, the bedrock of personal mastery, wields an omnipotent influence across multifaceted domains, exerting a pervasive impact on the trajectory of our lives. Within the intricate tapestry of our existence, it reigns supreme in what some refer to as the 'Big Four' domains—appetites, mental attitude, time, and even solitude.

Appetite, as a primal force, dwells deep within our being, often urging indulgence in excesses that pose a threat to our well-being. The siren call of overindulgence, whether in food and drink or the allure of substances detrimental to our health, can jeopardize our vitality and focus. The empirical evidence resonates profoundly, underscoring the paramount importance of self-discipline as an ever-vigilant guard against these perils. Beyond being a mere moral imperative, cultivating self-discipline in this sphere emerges as a pragmatic strategy—one that not only safeguards longevity but also sustains mental acuity, empowering individuals to navigate life's temptations with resilience and foresight.

Another bastion fortified by the pillars of self-discipline resides within the domain of nurturing a Positive Mental Attitude (PMA). This transcends the realm of positive thinking; it emerges as the fulcrum upon which the wheel of definitive goals pivots. This fortified mindset serves as a magnetic force, drawing in cooperation from others and beckoning the forces of faith and Infinite Intelligence. Here, self-discipline assumes the role of an adept architect, diligently shaping thoughts to attract desired outcomes and fortifying the mind against the encroachment of negativity—a resilient armor that shields the psyche amidst life's adversities, fostering resilience and unwavering resolve.

In these spheres and beyond, the omnipresence of self-discipline emerges as an essential attribute—an empowering force that transcends individual endeavors to forge a path toward holistic well-being and enduring success.

Time, the elusive currency of life, demands stringent discipline for optimal utilization. Wasting this invaluable asset in frivolous pursuits or idle chatter corrodes potential. An adage deems wasting time as sinful, highlighting its sacred value. The meticulous allocation of time, akin to financial budgeting, underscores the importance of a disciplined approach. The blueprint for the day, adhered to steadfastly, becomes a testament to the harnessing of time's power. The example of Solzhenitsyn echoes this sentiment profoundly, his unwavering discipline enabling him to endure the Gulag's horrors and wield his pen against injustice, even amidst exile.

Moreover, the often-underestimated domain of solitude unveils its profound transformative potential, intimately entwined with the fabric of self-discipline. Solitude isn't synonymous with mere isolation; it transcends mere physical seclusion, presenting itself as a deliberate and purposeful withdrawal from external distractions to foster profound introspection, creativity, and personal growth. It's a deliberate sanctuary that provides the fertile ground for the cultivation of deeper self-awareness and the nurturing of one's creative essence.

The renowned author Solzhenitsyn's deliberate retreat to a secluded town in Vermont offers a poignant illustration of the transformative power of solitude. In a world where fame and adulation beckoned, his disciplined pursuit of solitude served as a testament to the vital importance of crafting an environment conducive to deep reflection and focused output. Through this intentional seclusion, he not only honed his craft but also delved into the profound depths of his thoughts, birthing literary masterpieces that continue to resonate across generations.

In essence, these 'Big Four' pillars—appetites, mental attitude, time, and solitude—emerge as the sturdy foundation upon which the edifice of self-discipline stands tall. They transcend mere domains of control; they unfold as dynamic pathways for continual self-improvement, guiding individuals toward a more purposeful, resilient, and impactful existence. Each of these domains embodies a realm where self-discipline becomes the guiding light, illuminating the path towards a more profound understanding of oneself and the world, fostering an unwavering commitment to personal growth and fulfillment.

DEFINITENESS OF PURPOSE

Grasping the profound significance of a clear and resolute purpose should resonate as a foundational principle within the depths of your consciousness. It stands as not just a starting point but the North Star guiding every accomplishment, particularly when tethered to a robust and compelling motivation. If, by any chance, the contours of your definite purpose remain elusive, consider it a beckoning call to revisit earlier chapters—the stepping stones of your life's narrative. Seize the pen and let it dance upon the parchment, delineating with intricate detail your primary life objective, accompanied by a comprehensive blueprint meticulously crafted for its realization. This initial act transcends mere planning; it marks the inaugural stride into the illustrious realm of self-discipline—a profound commitment to charting a purpose-driven course. For even the boundless wisdom and guidance emanating from Infinite Intelligence may falter if the destination lacks the clarity and precision of your intent.

An anecdote surfaces, echoing this notion: a parable recounting the plight of a stranded preacher atop his church roof amid rising floodwaters. His fervent prayers for divine intervention echoed, yet when three boats appeared for rescue, the preacher, clinging to faith, dismissed each aid. The allegory crescendos tragically as the waters engulf the preacher, leading to an untimely demise. At the gates of heaven, inquisitive about his unfulfilled rescue, the preacher, faced with divine presence, questioned the reason for abandonment. The gentle yet pointed response rang clear: the boats were sent as opportunities for salvation, yet the preacher's lack of action led to tragic consequences.

The allegory reaches its tragic crescendo as the floodwaters overwhelm the preacher, leading to an untimely demise. In the solemn silence of the afterlife, standing at the gates of heaven, the preacher, perplexed by the unfulfilled rescue, inquired about the apparent abandonment. Faced with the divine presence, his query was met with a gentle yet poignant response: the boats sent were the opportunities for salvation, but the preacher's lack of action in embracing these lifelines led to the tragic consequences that ensued.

Here, self-discipline emerges as not merely a concept but a pivotal force—an inner impetus that propels one into action when opportunities present themselves. It stands as the unwavering resolve that compels individuals to grasp the lifelines thrown in critical moments of decision-making, ensuring that opportunities aren't squandered due to vacillation or an over-reliance on external intervention. It's this internal fortitude that drives one to leap into action when the defining moment arises, recognizing and seizing the chances for progress and transformation.

THE POWER OF SELF-DISCIPLINE

Power is often synonymous with wealth, authority, and possessions, and figures like Rockefeller or Trump usually spring to mind in discussions about influential individuals. However, a remarkable and divergent example exists—one that challenges this conventional association. Mahatma Gandhi, a man stripped of material possessions and riches, wielded an influence that surpassed that of many in his era. The astonishing reality of Gandhi's influence becomes more pronounced upon a closer examination of its origins, which diverged from the traditional understanding of power prevalent during the British Empire's rule.

Gandhi's impact wasn't grounded in the accumulation of wealth or conventional authority; instead, it emanated from a profound understanding and harnessing of moral and nonviolent power. Through meticulous, deliberate, and sustained efforts spanning many years, he orchestrated the systematic dismantling of the British Empire's control over India. His approach to power, rooted in nonviolent resistance and civil disobedience, stood as an enigma that confounded and eluded the understanding of the British government. Gandhi's power lay not in material riches but in his unwavering commitment to principles that transcended conventional notions of authority. His legacy remains a testament to the transformative potential of moral influence and nonviolent action, showcasing that true power often lies beyond the realm of material possessions or wealth.

The five sources to above mentioned power are:

1. **Definiteness of Purpose:** Gandhi's unwavering focus on freeing India served as the bedrock of his power. His clarity of purpose wasn't merely a personal aspiration; it was a grand vision for the nation. This unequivocal aim gave direction to his actions, uniting millions behind a single cause and presenting an unassailable front against the British Empire. His resolute vision for India's freedom became a rallying cry that unified a diverse population and steered the collective effort towards liberation.

2. **Going Beyond Expectations:** Gandhi's selfless dedication extended far beyond conventional expectations. His actions weren't driven by personal ambition or glory; they were motivated by an altruistic desire to uplift the masses. His readiness to make

immense sacrifices without seeking personal gain resonated deeply with people, amplifying his impact significantly. This selfless commitment endeared him to the masses and propelled his influence exponentially.

3. **Applied Faith:** Gandhi's unshakable belief in the inevitability of India's freedom fortified his determination. His unwavering faith in his cause and the absolute conviction that it was destined to succeed sustained his resolve. This unyielding faith not only propelled his determination but also allowed him to tap into profound wells of inspiration and guidance from what he termed as Infinite Intelligence.

4. **Mastermind Alliance:** Gandhi forged an unparalleled alliance of minds, bringing together millions toward a shared goal. Despite diverse backgrounds and education levels, this collective force shared an unwavering faith and fervent desire for India's liberation. The sheer magnitude of this united force, driven by a shared vision, created an indomitable entity that the British Empire struggled to counter effectively.

5. **Self-Discipline:** Gandhi's personal discipline formed the very essence of his leadership. Despite the immense power at his disposal, he chose simplicity, rejecting personal aggrandizement or misuse of authority. His adherence to a modest lifestyle exemplified his self-discipline, earning not just respect but also solidifying his credibility and trust among the people. His unwavering commitment to his cause, resisting temptations that could have veered him off course, showcased the depth of his self-discipline and further fortified his influence.

Gandhi's influence and power didn't emanate from traditional sources like wealth or material possessions. Instead, it stemmed from the unwavering strength of his character, his resolute commitment, and his extraordinary capacity to inspire and unite millions toward a common vision of liberation. His legacy serves as an enduring testament to the sheer potency of these unconventional sources of power when wielded with unwavering integrity and profound purpose.

His ability to galvanize people, not through coercion or force, but by appealing to their sense of justice and moral conscience, marked a unique and impactful form of leadership. Gandhi's power lay in his authenticity, a rare attribute that resonated deeply with people from all walks of life. He didn't leverage conventional authority or wield economic dominance; instead, he drew upon the moral authority derived from his principled actions and steadfast beliefs.

Moreover, Gandhi's commitment to nonviolent resistance showcased the immense influence of moral and ethical power. His philosophy of Satyagraha, rooted in truth and nonviolent protest, not only confronted oppression but also demonstrated the transformative force of moral persuasion. His methods served as a powerful reminder that ethical principles, when lived and practiced earnestly, possess an unparalleled ability to effect monumental societal change.

Gandhi's legacy epitomizes the enduring truth that genuine power doesn't always originate from external trappings or conventional sources. Instead, it emerges from the authenticity of character, steadfast adherence to principles, and the ability to inspire collective action toward a noble cause. His life remains a poignant example of how unwavering integrity and a clear, purposeful vision can transcend material wealth and wield a profound, lasting influence on the world.

4

ORGANIZED PLANNING

Napoleon Hill

No individual possesses an exhaustive blend of experience, education, inherent skills, and knowledge requisite for amassing significant wealth without the collaboration and support of others. Each strategy crafted in your pursuit of accumulating riches ought to stem from a collective effort involving not just your own ideas but also the insights and contributions of your Master Mind Group. While you may conceive plans independently, it's crucial to ensure these strategies undergo scrutiny and endorsement by the members of your alliance.

Should your initial plan falter in achieving success, it becomes imperative to substitute it with a new, refined blueprint. Persistence in this iterative process of trial and adjustment is paramount. Many falter precisely at this juncture, lacking the perseverance required to forge new plans when the initial ones prove ineffective.

Even the most astute and intelligent individual will flounder in their quest for wealth or in any endeavor without practical, viable plans. Understanding this, it's crucial to bear in mind that setbacks are not synonymous with permanent failure. They merely signal a need for reassessment and recalibration of plans. Take inspiration from Thomas A. Edison, who encountered temporary defeat a staggering 10,000 times before finally perfecting the incandescent electric light bulb—an emblematic testament to persistence in the face of adversity.

Temporary setbacks ought to serve as a beacon, indicating the necessity to reassess and refine your strategy. Countless individuals endure lives marked by hardship and impoverishment due to the absence of a sound, well-structured plan for wealth accumulation. Hence, the key lies in perpetually revisiting, revising, and reconstructing plans until discovering the one that yields success.

Henry Ford's amassed fortune wasn't solely attributed to innate brilliance but was instead the product of his steadfast adherence to a sound and meticulous plan. Comparatively, countless individuals may boast superior educations compared to Ford, yet their lives are mired in poverty due to the absence of a well-structured strategy for wealth accumulation.

The magnitude of your accomplishments is inextricably tied to the quality and robustness of your plans. While this might sound like a fundamental truth, its significance cannot be overstated. One doesn't face defeat until they concede internally, allowing setbacks to appear insurmountable. It's a truth reiterated often, primarily because it's all too easy to succumb to defeat at the initial signs of adversity.

Consider James J. Hill, who initially grappled with temporary defeat while striving to secure capital for constructing a transcontinental railroad. Despite this setback, Hill emerged triumphant by engineering new plans, ultimately turning defeat into victory. Similarly, Henry Ford encountered setbacks not only at the onset of his automobile career but even when he was well on his way to the summit. Yet, his resilience prevailed as he continually innovated new strategies, forging ahead towards financial success.

The stories of those who've amassed significant wealth often gloss over the arduous battles and temporary defeats they encountered en route to their triumphs. We tend to perceive only their ultimate victories, disregarding the setbacks and challenges they had to overcome before "making it."

No adherent to this philosophy should expect to amass a substantial fortune without encountering transient setbacks. When confronted with defeat, it serves as a signal—a beacon illuminating the insufficiency or inefficiency of your current plans. It's an opportunity to reconstruct, fortify, and refine those plans, propelling yourself once more toward the coveted objective. Should you surrender before reaching your goal, you take on the unfortunate label of a quitter. Remember, a quitter never tastes victory, while a persistent pursuer never relinquishes their pursuit. Embed this maxim deeply within your consciousness; inscribe it boldly, in inch-high letters, where your eyes meet it each night before slumber and every morning before embarking on your day's endeavors.

When assembling your Master Mind Group, seek out individuals who don't perceive defeat as an insurmountable barrier. Their resilience and refusal to capitulate in the face of setbacks will add invaluable strength to your collective pursuit.

There exists a misguided belief among some that money alone begets more money. However, the truth lies in the transformation of DESIRE into its monetary equivalent through the principles outlined herein. Money itself remains an inert entity, devoid of action or thought. Yet, it responds when beckoned by the fervent call of DESIRE. It's this transmutation, this channeling of longing into a tangible force, that summons money forth.

PLANNING THE SALE OF SERVICES

This chapter delves into the intricate strategies and methods to market personal services, offering invaluable guidance for anyone seeking to promote their unique skill set. While this information holds practical significance for those already engaged in marketing their services, its value transcends mere practicality. It stands as an indispensable guide for those nurturing aspirations of leadership within their respective vocations.

Success in the pursuit of accumulating wealth hinges upon astute and meticulous planning. The upcoming pages unfurl comprehensive instructions tailored for individuals commencing their journey towards riches through the sale of personal services. It's worthwhile to note that the genesis of numerous colossal fortunes traces back to compensation for personal services rendered or the monetization of groundbreaking ideas. For individuals possessing limited property, ideas and personal services become the invaluable currency exchanged for wealth.

In the broad spectrum of humanity, there exist two archetypes: Leaders and Followers. An important decision lies in delineating whether one aims to ascend to leadership within their domain or opt to perpetually follow. The chasm in compensation between a leader and a follower is immense. While there is no disgrace in adopting the role of a follower initially, there's little credit in remaining entrenched in that role indefinitely. Remarkably, most renowned leaders commenced their journeys as followers, eventually ascending to greatness due to their astute ability to be intelligent followers. It's noteworthy that a proficient leader often emerges from the ranks of an intelligent follower.

Being an astute follower isn't merely a stepping stone; it

comes with a plethora of advantages, notably the opportunity to glean knowledge from the leader. The adept follower doesn't just follow blindly but engages intelligently, seizing the chance to acquire wisdom and insight from their leader, nurturing their own potential for future leadership.

THE 11 MAJOR FACTORS OF LEADERSHIP

These attributes collectively define effective leadership, showcasing a blend of personal traits and professional competencies essential for guiding and inspiring others toward shared objectives:

1. **Unwavering Courage Rooted in Self-Knowledge:** Leadership isn't just about courage; it's a blend of courage and profound self-awareness. A leader's courage, cultivated through deep self-knowledge and expertise in their field, serves as a magnetic force for followers. They naturally gravitate towards leaders exuding confidence and steadfast courage. An intelligent follower seeks assurance in their leader, and a deficiency in self-assurance can swiftly erode a leader's credibility and influence.
2. **Self-Control as a Demonstrative Force:** The bedrock of a leader's influence lies in their self-discipline. It's not just about controlling oneself but setting an example for others. This self-discipline becomes a beacon for followers, especially the discerning ones who mirror and learn from these traits, shaping a disciplined and focused team.
3. **A Keen Sense of Justice:** Justice and fairness serve as cornerstones of a leader's credibility and followers'

respect. Without these ethical pillars, a leader's ability to command trust crumbles. Upholding fairness doesn't just earn respect; it fosters an environment of integrity and mutual trust, essential for sustained leadership.

4. **Definiteness of Decision:** A leader's decisiveness provides direction and clarity for their team. Indecision in leadership signals uncertainty, causing doubt among followers regarding the direction and capabilities of their leader.
5. **Definiteness of Plans:** Successful leaders don't just rely on inspiration; they meticulously plan their endeavors. Operating without concrete plans is akin to steering a ship without a rudder—leading inevitably to chaos and failure. Leaders' thorough planning and execution set the foundation for their team's success.
6. **Exceeding Expectations:** True leadership entails surpassing expectations. Leaders don't just demand excellence; they embody it. This commitment to outperforming expectations inspires dedication and commitment among followers.
7. **A Pleasing Personality:** A leader's demeanor significantly influences team dynamics. Commanding respect requires a demeanor that exudes professionalism and care. A careless appearance undermines a leader's credibility, hindering effective communication and collaboration.
8. **Sympathy and Understanding:** Empathy towards followers' challenges and a deep understanding of their experiences forge strong connections. Effective leaders resonate with their team's struggles, fostering a supportive environment and trust.
9. **Mastery of Detail:** Effective leadership hinges on a

leader's comprehensive understanding of their position. Mastery of intricate details ensures informed decisions and guides the team towards success.
10. **Assuming Responsibility:** Leaders shoulder the weight of their team's successes and failures. Accepting responsibility, rather than shifting blame, strengthens a leader's credibility and fortifies team morale.
11. **Cooperative Approach:** Leadership isn't solitary; it thrives on cooperative efforts. Leaders must foster a culture of cooperation, harnessing collective power to achieve shared goals. Encouraging teamwork and cooperation among followers empowers the team and magnifies the impact of leadership.

Leadership, in its essence, embodies two distinct paradigms: the first, and notably effective, is leadership fostered through the willing consent and genuine empathy of followers. Conversely, the alternative approach, typified by leadership enforced through coercion and imposition, lacks the essential elements of willing consent and empathy from followers, making it inherently less effective and considerably less sustainable over time.

Across the annals of history, myriad examples spotlight the inherent fragility of leadership rooted in force. The inevitable downfall of dictators and monarchs throughout various epochs stands as a resounding testament to the transience of authoritarian rule. These historical vignettes consistently underscore a universal truth: people are inherently reluctant to indefinitely submit to leadership thrust upon them by sheer force.

The contemporary landscape, amidst its socio-political and economic complexities, marks the inception of a distinct era in the intricate dynamics between leaders and their followers. This evolving epoch distinctly demands a novel breed of leaders—individuals keenly attuned to a paradigm of leadership deeply rooted in collaboration and cooperation. Those tethered to the archaic methodology of leadership by force find themselves at a crossroads, necessitating an urgent adaptation to this emerging ethos of cooperation. Failure to align with this evolving landscape risks relegating such leaders to the ranks of mere followers, as there seems to be no viable alternative pathway within this transformative and cooperative paradigm.

The evolving landscape of the business world heralds a significant transformation in the dynamics between employers and employees, leaders and followers. A paradigm shift is underway, envisioning an alliance founded on mutual collaboration and the equitable sharing of business gains. This heralds a departure from the traditional hierarchical structures towards a model grounded in partnership and shared success. Drawing lessons from the tumultuous histories of fallen despots, there's a chilling parallel visible in contemporary business, finance, and labor leaders in America. Their authoritative and autocratic approaches, reminiscent of historical autocrats, are swiftly becoming obsolete within the evolving narrative of leadership.

This shifting landscape underscores the rising significance of leadership rooted in consent—an approach built upon the collective will and endorsement of followers. It stands as the linchpin of sustainable leadership models, resonating deeply in a world that increasingly values cooperation, mutual respect, and fair partnerships between leaders and their teams.

Human nature inherently resists forced leadership. While compliance under duress might be achieved momentarily, the genuine willingness to follow isn't sustainable under coercive regimes. This intrinsic resistance underscores the urgency for a departure from these antiquated methods, steering towards a new paradigm that champions collaboration, inclusivity, and a more democratic form of leadership.

The emerging paradigm of leadership not only encapsulates the 11 Major Factors elucidated in this chapter but also envisions the assimilation of additional yet-to-be-identified factors. Leaders anchoring their styles in these foundational principles will find themselves well-equipped to lead across diverse domains of life.

The intricate and protracted economic challenges that have gripped the global landscape can be largely attributed to the absence of this modern brand of leadership. The scarcity of adept leaders capable of navigating these complexities has exacerbated the global predicaments. Consequently, there's an amplified demand for leaders well-versed in the application of these innovative leadership methodologies, surpassing the current pool of such leaders. While some leaders from the traditional echelons might endeavor to reform and adapt to this new style, the prevalent narrative strongly suggests the pressing need for an influx of fresh leadership.

Amidst this imperative for a new paradigm of leadership lies a ripe opportunity, one that could potentially be yours to seize. As the world clamors for leaders embodying these progressive principles, those primed to adopt and champion this contemporary ethos stand on the cusp of a substantial opportunity for personal and professional growth. This transformative phase in leadership represents a gateway to a new era of influence and impact, offering a chance to redefine and shape the future landscape of leadership.

THE 11 MAJOR CAUSES OF FAILURE IN LEADERSHIP

Each of these failures can significantly impact leadership effectiveness, acting as potential stumbling blocks that hinder a leader's success. Hill's insights offer a nuanced understanding of the qualities and behaviors indispensable for effective leadership, while concurrently cautioning against these common pitfalls. By illuminating these potential stumbling blocks, Hill not only highlights the significance of avoiding these pitfalls but also underscores the importance of cultivating a leadership style that navigates through these challenges with resilience and adaptability:

1. **Inability to Organize Details**: The hallmark of effective leadership isn't solely about guiding from a distance but also mastering the minutiae of every endeavor. Genuine leaders don't let the demands of leadership eclipse their attention to detail. Their commitment to meticulous oversight doesn't simply involve ticking boxes on a project plan. It transcends that; true leaders actively engage in execution, understanding that plans are dynamic and require ongoing adaptation. They exhibit organizational proficiency coupled with the art of adept task delegation. It's not just about assigning tasks but ensuring that each component contributes meaningfully to the larger vision.
2. **Abdicating Responsibility vs. Delegating**: Delegation isn't a mere task assignment; it's a refined skill requiring trust, guidance, and empowerment. It's strategic, considering individual strengths and areas for development. Abdication, however, dismisses these considerations, leading to task-shuffling without regard for capabilities or follow-up. Genuine leaders don't just delegate; they foster growth and proficiency by delegating responsibilities with mentorship and

support. They aim to cultivate a sense of ownership and skill enhancement in their team.

3. **Unwillingness to Render Humble Service**: True leaders exemplify the principle of leading by example. Their strong work ethic extends beyond delegating tasks; they willingly undertake any job assigned to others. This demonstration asserts that leadership isn't about wielding authority but embodies solidarity and shared responsibility. When leaders expect more from their team than they are willing to contribute themselves, it not only undermines effective leadership but also adversely impacts team morale.

4. **Expectation of Pay for Knowledge, Not Action**: Hill's insight challenges the misconception that tenure, qualifications, or connections warrant greater compensation or respect. Genuine leadership isn't just about possessing knowledge but practically applying that knowledge. Effective leaders comprehend that action, along with the ability to motivate and guide others, are the real currencies of leadership. It's not about titles or credentials; it's about what one accomplishes and the inspiration they evoke in others to achieve.

5. **Fear of Competition from Followers**: A leader's apprehension about being overshadowed by their team members can stifle the growth and innovation potential within the team. This fear often leads to a reluctance to empower individuals fully or recognize their strengths. However, genuine leaders approach this differently. They actively cultivate an environment where individual talents are not only encouraged but celebrated. They understand that by nurturing the

unique abilities of each team member and fostering collaborative efforts, not only does the team excel, but the leader's effectiveness also elevates. They recognize that a team's success reflects positively on the leader's ability to nurture and guide.

6. **Lack of Imagination**: Imagination is a cornerstone of effective leadership, not just a nice-to-have attribute. True leaders embrace adaptability, creativity, and forward-thinking as essential components for navigating complexities and envisioning innovative solutions. Unfortunately, some project managers adhere strictly to rigid methodologies, failing to acknowledge that projects are dynamic and often require agile, imaginative thinking to address unexpected challenges. Leaders who lack imagination limit their potential to explore alternative strategies and innovative approaches, potentially hindering the team's adaptability and hindering the path to success.

7. **Selfishness**: A leader's self-centered approach can have detrimental effects on team cohesion and morale. Genuine leaders understand the significance of shared successes in fostering a stronger, more motivated team. They exhibit selflessness by deflecting the spotlight from themselves and acknowledging and celebrating their team's contributions. By doing so, they cultivate a culture of mutual appreciation and motivation, where every team member feels valued and recognized for their efforts.

8. **Intemperance**: Hill's counsel against overindulgence underscores the need for focus and resilience in leadership. Effective leaders maintain clarity and energy by avoiding excessive indulgence in various pleasures.

This moderation ensures that their endurance and vitality remain uncompromised, allowing them to sustain their focus and drive towards their goals. By exercising temperance, leaders exemplify discipline and self-control, setting a precedent for their team members to follow suit.

9. **Disloyalty**: The bedrock of effective leadership is trust. When leaders fail to extend trust and show respect to their team members, it breeds an atmosphere of doubt and suspicion. Such actions risk eroding the very foundation upon which effective collaboration and cooperation thrive. In contrast, loyalty among team members bolsters a leader's credibility and fortifies the commitment of the team towards collective success. Leaders who prioritize and foster loyalty within their teams cultivate an environment where trust becomes the cornerstone of their leadership.

10. **Emphasis on "Authority" of Leadership**: Genuine leadership transcends the notion of authority through fear or dominance. It's not about commanding compliance but inspiring genuine dedication and respect through encouragement and mutual respect. Leaders who resort to intimidation tactics may gain temporary compliance, yet they often fail to instill true commitment or respect within their teams. Authentic leadership isn't rooted in fear but in building an environment where every team member feels valued, heard, and respected, fostering an atmosphere conducive to innovation and growth.

11. **Overemphasis on Title**: The essence of leadership lies beyond titles or positions; it resides in one's character, actions, and the integrity they uphold. True leaders

don't rely on titles to command respect; instead, they earn it through their authenticity, ethical conduct, and the trust they instill in others. They create an open-door policy not because of their titles but because of the genuine connections they establish and the culture of trust and collaboration they foster. They recognize that genuine leadership authority doesn't stem from a position on an organizational chart but from the quality of their interactions and the example they set for others to follow.

The ramifications of each of these failures reverberate profoundly through the realm of leadership effectiveness. Hill's invaluable insights meticulously underscore the intrinsic qualities and nuanced behaviors imperative for steering effective leadership. His discerning observations serve as a poignant cautionary guide, illuminating the treacherous pitfalls that, if left unchecked, pose formidable barriers to a leader's triumphant journey towards success. These insights, honed through meticulous observation and study, serve as a beacon, urging leaders to navigate the complex terrain of leadership with vigilance, eschewing the detrimental patterns that can undermine their ability to inspire, guide, and propel their teams towards collective achievement.

EIGHT MUSTS FOR AN EFFECTIVE RESUME

Creating an effective resume demands a level of attention to detail similar to a lawyer meticulously preparing a case for trial in court. For individuals navigating the intricate art of resume crafting without extensive experience, seeking guidance from a professional becomes essential. Just as successful merchants engage experts adept in the art and psychology of advertising to eloquently showcase the virtues of their products, individuals offering personal services for hire should take a similar approach. Strategically presenting and compellingly articulating one's skills and experiences, much like marketing a product, can significantly bolster the likelihood of making a lasting impression and securing opportunities in today's fiercely competitive job market.

In an era where the job market is ever-evolving and intensely competitive, the necessity of a compelling resume cannot be overstated. It's not just a document detailing one's qualifications and experiences; it's a marketing tool designed to captivate potential employers' attention. Similar to how an advertisement is meticulously crafted to appeal to consumers, a resume serves as an advertisement for an individual's skills, accomplishments, and potential contributions to a company or organization.

For someone unaccustomed to the intricacies of resume crafting, navigating this terrain can be daunting. Engaging the expertise of a professional in the field can be likened to hiring a seasoned advertising specialist. Their guidance and insight can transform a mundane resume into a compelling narrative that not only conveys qualifications but also captures the essence of one's professional journey and aspirations.

Approaching resume building as a form of marketing strategy allows individuals to showcase their unique value proposition effectively. Just as a well-crafted advertisement entices consumers to purchase a product, a skillfully tailored resume entices employers to consider and hire a candidate. In today's competitive job market, the power of a well-crafted resume cannot be underestimated—it can be the key that unlocks doors to fulfilling career opportunities.

1. **Education and Specialization:** The core essence of a resume thrives on portraying the rich tapestry of one's educational odyssey. It's more than a mere listing of attained degrees; it's a narrative that should intricately weave in the specific subjects pursued and the rationale guiding those choices. Unveiling the motivations behind these academic pursuits not only showcases a deliberate path of learning but also illustrates a holistic approach to personal and professional growth, emphasizing the fusion of passion, skill acquisition, and future aspirations.

2. **Comprehensive Experience: A Profound Dive into Past Roles:** Dive into the depths of relevant experience, painting a vivid picture of the professional voyage that aligns with the desired role. Offer a narrative that transcends mere job titles, expounding upon the intricacies of past roles. Illuminate the responsibilities shouldered, the milestones achieved, and the transformative impact created. It's pivotal to not just name former employers and their locations but to craft a narrative that encapsulates the evolution of your career, showcasing the amalgamation of experiences that uniquely equip you for the coveted role. Elevate the exceptional moments, those unique experiences that have honed your skills and perspectives, aligning perfectly with the sought-after position.

3. **References and Recommendations: Testimonials of Trustworthiness:** Acknowledge the pivotal role of robust references in fortifying the credibility of your candidacy. Beyond attaching photocopies, provide condensed yet impactful excerpts from commendations by former employers, influential educators, and

respected personalities. These testimonials serve as pillars of trust, illuminating your character, competence, and the invaluable contributions you've made in various spheres.

4. **Inclusion of a Photograph: Adding a Human Touch:** Embedding a recent, unmounted photograph or a professionally reproduced one goes beyond the conventional resume. It infuses a human element, transcending the paper-and-ink narrative to establish a more personal and relatable connection. A well-placed image can resonate with the employer, offering a glimpse of the person behind the qualifications, fostering an immediate sense of familiarity and rapport.

5. **Specific Position Application: Precision in Aspiration:** Precision reigns supreme when delineating the coveted position. Clearly articulate the precise role coveted, showcasing a lucid understanding of your specialized skill set and its seamless alignment with the role's demands. Envision a symbiotic relationship between your expertise and the requirements of the role, allowing your qualifications to shine within the specific context of the desired position.

6. **Qualifications Alignment: The Nexus of Skills and Role Demands:** Dedicate substantial discourse to spotlighting the harmony between your qualifications and the distinct requirements of the desired position. Articulate with granularity how your unique skill set and experiential arsenal intricately merge to carve an ideal candidate profile. Offer a narrative that seamlessly marries your competencies with the nuanced demands of the role, presenting yourself as the perfect fit.

7. **Offering Probationary Work: Displaying Confidence**

Through Action: Ponder the proposition of a probationary period, a bold yet impactful gesture showcasing unwavering commitment and self-assurance. This unconventional offer substantiates your determination to add tangible value to the organization. Express your readiness to substantiate your capabilities, transforming this period of evaluation into a testament of your potential contributions. By exhibiting confidence in your abilities and the conviction to secure the role, this offer substantiates your sincerity and competence.

8. **Understanding the Prospective Employer: Beyond the Surface Connection:** Illuminate the depth of effort invested in understanding the essence of the prospective employer's business. Your resume should exude the fruits of meticulous research, showcasing a profound comprehension of the company's ethos, industry dynamics, and future trajectories. This display of insights serves as a testament to your proactive engagement and genuine interest in not just the role but the organization's journey, indicating your potential to seamlessly integrate into their vision and mission.

Moreover, remember the power of presentation. A meticulously crafted resume not only reflects your qualifications but also showcases your meticulous nature. There have been instances where resumes, meticulously designed and presented, catapulted applicants into employment without the need for a face-to-face interview. The visual appeal and attention to detail in these documents spoke volumes about the applicant's character and dedication.

When considering the success of a lawyer in court, it's

not solely their exhaustive knowledge of the law that secures a win; it's the meticulous preparation and presentation of the case that decisively tilts the scales in their favor. Likewise, in the competitive arena of job applications, an impeccably prepared resume holds the key to victory. Its depth, thoroughness, and quality create the foundational advantage that positions you favorably even before the selection process begins.

Never underestimate the power of elaboration on your resume; employers hunger for detailed insights into well-qualified candidates as fervently as you seek employment. The reality is that the triumph of many prosperous employers significantly relies on their ability to handpick highly qualified team members. They crave every minute detail and piece of relevant information that could potentially distinguish one applicant from another in the pool of candidates.

Much like a lawyer meticulously builds a case, a carefully crafted resume serves as your compelling case for employment. It's a chance to present a comprehensive narrative that encapsulates your qualifications, experiences, and unique value proposition. Employers seek depth and substance in resumes; they're searching for candidates who can not only fulfill roles but also add distinct value to their organizations.

In today's competitive job market, a resume isn't just a document; it's your ticket to being noticed and considered. Detailing your skills, experiences, and accomplishments isn't a show of verbosity; it's a strategic approach to providing a clear and comprehensive picture of your potential contributions. Employers appreciate the effort taken to articulate your qualifications thoroughly—it demonstrates your commitment and seriousness towards the application process, setting you apart in the eyes of prospective employers.

Just as successful salespeople meticulously groom themselves, understanding the lasting impression of a first encounter, your resume stands as your emissary in the job market. It's your sales representative in print, and dressing it in an impressive 'attire' will ensure it stands out boldly amidst a sea of applications. If the position you aspire to is of genuine value, it warrants a meticulous pursuit. Moreover, presenting yourself uniquely to employers can lead to a more lucrative offer right from the outset, setting you apart from the traditional application crowd.

Should you opt for an employment agency in your job hunt, ensure they not only understand but also champion the detailed representation of your qualifications. A comprehensive, well-crafted resume that aligns with the aforementioned criteria can significantly elevate your standing both with the agency and potential employers, setting you on a distinctive pedestal among other candidates.

HOW TO GET THE EXACT POSITION YOU DESIRE

The intrinsic joy of work is deeply intertwined with a person's innate talents and passions. For instance, an artist finds solace and fulfillment in wielding paints to create vibrant masterpieces, while a craftsman discovers their calling in the tactile artistry of shaping materials with skilled hands. Similarly, a writer's heart sings with every stroke of the pen or tap of the keyboard, finding pure delight in the creation of narratives and stories.

However, not everyone possesses clearly defined talents. For those with less distinct inclinations, preferences often lean towards specific fields within the vast spectrum of business and industry. This diversity of skills and preferences is where America excels—its tapestry of occupations spans the entire spectrum, from the earthy roots of tilling the soil and the intricate mechanisms of manufacturing, to the artistry of marketing, the intricacies of commerce, and the specialized realms of the professions.

The brilliance of America lies not just in the diversity of its occupational offerings but also in the embrace of individual inclinations and talents, allowing each person to find their niche and contribute their unique essence to the vibrant mosaic of the workforce. This rich assortment of vocations ensures that individuals can align their skills and passions with a plethora of opportunities, fostering a society where each person's distinct abilities are recognized, valued, and harnessed for collective advancement.

1. **Defining Your Desired Job**: Initiating your job search involves intricately defining the kind of role that resonates with your skills and passions. This clear articulation, succinctly put in writing, serves as a compass, not just clarifying your aspirations but also leaving space for the potential creation of a role within a company if it doesn't currently exist. It's about not only identifying what you want but also envisioning what the perfect role would entail based on your abilities and ambitions.

2. **Targeted Selection**: Precision in your job search extends to identifying a specific company or even an individual within an organization where you aspire to work. This deliberate targeting ensures that your efforts are focused and aligned with a particular entity that mirrors your values, culture preferences, and long-term professional goals. Directing your attention to a specific company allows for more tailored applications and connections, enhancing the relevance of your candidacy.

3. **Thorough Employer Research**: Thoroughly acquainting yourself with your prospective employer goes beyond skimming the surface. It involves delving deep into understanding their organizational structure, company culture, mission, values, and growth trajectory. This knowledge empowers you to tailor your approach and offerings to align seamlessly with the company's ethos and objectives, positioning yourself as an informed and enthusiastic candidate who genuinely fits within their framework.
4. **Self-Analysis and Offering**: Conducting a comprehensive analysis of your own talents and capabilities is foundational. It's about understanding not just what you do but also what sets you apart. Determining the unique value you can bring to the table enables you to strategize on leveraging these strengths. Your aim is to provide distinct advantages, innovative services, developmental strategies, or groundbreaking ideas that you're confident about delivering successfully. This analysis informs your offering, highlighting what makes you an invaluable asset to any prospective employer.
5. **Shifting Focus: Giving Instead of Just Seeking:** Redirecting your job search strategy from merely seeking "a job" to focusing on what you can offer is pivotal. Shifting away from the traditional approach of asking, "Do you have a job for me?" and instead concentrating on what value you can contribute to the prospective employer showcases your proactive mindset. It's about highlighting how you can actively contribute to their success rather than passively seeking opportunities.

6. **Professional Presentation**: Once you've meticulously crafted your strategy, collaborating with an experienced writer or career coach is beneficial. Their expertise ensures that your comprehensive plan is encapsulated in a well-structured, detailed document. This professional representation not only enhances the clarity and coherence of your strategy but also ensures that it's presented in an appealing, organized, and impactful manner that catches the attention of prospective employers.

7. **Presentation and Confidence in Action**: Finally, presenting your comprehensive plan to the relevant authority within the company demands confidence and finesse. Your preparation, thoroughness, and confident presentation will speak volumes about your dedication and expertise. Companies are continually seeking individuals who bring substantial value. A well-defined action plan, specifically tailored to benefit the company, positions you as an asset that can contribute meaningfully to their growth and success, standing out among other candidates.

While this approach might demand a slightly extended timeline for execution, the potential benefits it promises in terms of income, career advancement, and gaining acknowledgment are substantial. Investing additional time upfront can serve as a shortcut, potentially bypassing years spent in lower-paying positions. Its advantages are manifold, primarily in compressing the timeline for achieving desired goals. Often, this strategy condenses what might typically take anywhere from one to five years into a significantly shorter span, accelerating career growth and progression.

Imagine this: Every individual who begins their professional journey or steps into the career landscape at a mid-level point on the ladder does so not by mere coincidence, but through careful and calculated planning. They meticulously map out their trajectory, identifying opportunities, and crafting a roadmap toward their aspirations. This deliberate approach to career advancement and entry into the professional realm, barring instances where favoritism or nepotism come into play, underscores the importance of thoughtful strategy and meticulous planning in propelling oneself forward in their career journey.

Delving deeper into this approach unveils its multifaceted advantages. Beyond merely securing a higher salary or quicker career progression, it offers intangible benefits. It cultivates a deeper understanding of the industry landscape, hones strategic skills, and nurtures a proactive mindset geared toward seizing opportunities. It's not merely about entering the workforce but about making a meaningful and impactful entry aligned with one's long-term career objectives.

5

POSITIVE MENTAL ATTITUDE

Napoleon Hill

Let me tell you something that happened last Saturday. I went down to the travel agency to get my ticket changed so I could come back on Monday instead of Sunday. When I walked in, the manager of the travel agency grabbed my hand when he saw who I was, and he introduced himself and started in to selling me *Think and Grow Rich*. While he was holding my hand and talking to me, along came a friend of his who was connected with one of the airlines. When his friend heard the name Napoleon Hill, he grabbed the other hand and started to sell me *Think and Grow Rich*. He said, "You may be interested in knowing that before I went with the airline, I had a sales organization with approximately a hundred people, and I required every salesman to have all of your books. That was a must." Well, I felt pretty good. Outside, I encountered two very nice-looking young ladies standing on the sidewalk, giving out election literature.

As I passed by, one of them said, "Aren't you Napoleon Hill? I was at a woman's club about two years ago when you delivered an address. This is my cousin. Both of our husbands are very successful now due to the fact they have read your books." I went on over to my car, and a policeman was making out a ticket. After all this talk, there was a payoff. You see, I put a penny in the parking meter, thinking that twelve minutes would be all I would need on the meter. But as I stopped to bathe my vanity in all this nice conversation, when I got to the meter, a policeman was halfway finished making out a ticket. He didn't know whose car it was, but I walked up to him and said, "Now, you wouldn't do that to Napoleon Hill, would you?" He said,

"Who?" I said, "Napoleon Hill." He said, "No, I wouldn't do that to Napoleon Hill, but I certainly would do it to you." I showed him my credit card and my driver's license. And he said, "Well, I'll be a monkey's uncle!" He took the ticket and tore it up and said we'd just forget about that. And he said, "You may be interested in knowing that I'm on the Glendale Police Force as a result of reading your book, *Think and Grow Rich*."

Nothing constructive and worthy of man's efforts ever has been or ever will be achieved, except that which comes from a positive mental attitude based on definiteness of purpose, activated by a burning desire, and intensified until the burning desire is elevated to the plane of applied faith.

The following outlines five distinct mental states that lay the groundwork for fostering a positive mental attitude. In simpler terms, these five elements serve as prerequisites for cultivating and nurturing a positive mindset: aspirations, expectations, passionate determination, practiced belief, and proactive engagement. These facets collectively pave the path toward embracing a constructive and optimistic outlook on life:

1. **Begin with Wishes:** At the outset, wishes reside within everyone's reservoir of desires. They are the whispers of our heart, articulating our desires for various

outcomes and possibilities. Yet, merely wishing for something seldom propels tangible action or manifests any substantial change. It's akin to tossing coins into a well and hoping for miracles without actively pursuing them. The passivity inherent in wishful thinking often leads to a standstill, where desires linger in the realm of dreams, waiting to be breathed into reality.

A step beyond wishes often veers into the realm of idle curiosity. This phase marks a transition from passive desires to a somewhat aimless exploration. Curiosity is indeed a splendid trait, but when left to wander aimlessly, it merely consumes time without yielding meaningful results. It's the idle pondering over the lives of others, whether neighbors or competitors, without any purposeful intent or actionable outcomes. While curiosity can be a catalyst for growth when harnessed effectively, when it spirals into idle musings, it fails to contribute to a positive mental attitude.

Therefore, while wishes might lay the groundwork for aspirations, progressing beyond idle curiosity and aimless musings becomes imperative to steer one's mental attitude toward proactive and purposeful endeavors.

2. **Wishes Lead to Hope:** Progressing beyond mere wishes leads one to the realm of hope, where desires assume a more tangible and defined shape. These hopes transform aspirations into more structured and purposeful expectations—hopes of achievements, aspirations of attaining goals, dreams of accomplishments, and desires for the accumulation of desired possessions or experiences. Yet, while hopes represent a step forward from wishes, harboring hopes

alone doesn't guarantee success. Simply hoping for success does not necessarily materialize it.

Indeed, hopes are an elevated form of aspirations, encapsulating a more determined outlook towards desired outcomes. However, not everyone who holds onto hopes achieves their desired goals. The distinction lies in the realization that hoping, while more purposeful than mere wishing, requires a further leap—transmuting hopes into the powerful realm of faith.

The essence of hope lies in its transformative potential. It serves as the conduit between desire and faith, marking the beginning of a transition. Unlike wishes that remain in the realm of desire, hope initiates a shift toward faith. It marks the evolution from a passive yearning to a more proactive and determined mindset. The difference between hope and wish lies in this crucial pivot—hope sets the stage for embracing faith.

Converting hopes into faith represents a profound mental shift. It's a transition from mere longing to an unwavering belief, a precursor to a state of mind characterized by conviction and confidence. This progression signifies the journey from a mere desire for something to the unshakable assurance that it can be achieved.

3. **Hope Fuels Burning Desire:** Beyond hope lies the transformative phase of a burning desire, marking a significant escalation in one's mental attitude. This transition represents a pivotal shift from mere hopes to an intensified, purpose-driven yearning. The distinction between a burning desire and a regular one lies in its fervor—an intensified longing that springs from the amalgamation of hope and unwavering determination.

A burning desire isn't just a fleeting wish; it's an obsessional, all-consuming passion, ignited by a fervent motive or multiple motives that propel one forward. It's not simply desiring something; it's a compelling force that emerges from a definitive sense of purpose. The potency of a burning desire hinges on the depth of motives that underpin it. The more motives aligned with a specific goal, the swifter emotions transmute into the fiery intensity of a burning desire.

Yet, even as one harnesses this fiery passion, there's another essential mental state critical to ensuring success. This phase transcends the realm of a burning desire and lays the groundwork for what comes next—an evolution of the mind that serves as a precursor to assured success.

4. **Applied Faith:** When you've transcended wishes, idle curiosity, hopes, and even a burning desire, you ascend to a higher mental realm known as applied faith. But what sets applied faith apart from ordinary belief in things?

    Applied faith represents an elevated form of belief—it's not merely believing in something but actively applying that belief to your actions and decisions. It's an intentional, purposeful alignment of your beliefs with your actions and endeavors. Unlike ordinary belief, which might be passive or theoretical, applied faith is dynamic and proactive. It's the embodiment of faith in action.

    The key distinction lies in the implementation aspect—applied faith isn't just about acknowledging or believing in certain principles or outcomes. It's about channeling that belief into concrete actions, decisions, and behaviors. It's the unwavering commitment to integrate your beliefs into every facet of your life, aligning your thoughts, actions, and attitudes toward the fulfillment of your objectives. Applied faith isn't confined to mere mental acceptance; it manifests as a deliberate, purpose-driven application of those beliefs in your daily conduct and pursuits.

5. **Action:** In essence, the term "applied" intricately intertwines with the concept of action. One could even consider it synonymous with active faith. Applied faith and active faith converge on a singular principle: faith propelled into motion, where belief finds expression through deliberate action—actions that align with one's convictions and beliefs. It signifies a conscious choice to not just hold beliefs but to actively live them out.

   When faith is translated into action, it becomes a potent force for change. Consider prayer, for instance; its efficacy often lies in the expression of a positive mental attitude. Effective prayers are not merely uttered words but emerge from individuals who've habituated their minds to consistently dwell in a positive mental space. It's the fusion of faith with action, where prayers are not passive requests but active manifestations of a positive mental attitude.

   Therefore, the transformational power lies not just in the act of faith or belief but in the active, purposeful translation of those beliefs into actionable steps. It's this alignment between faith and action that unleashes the true potential for transformative results and positive outcomes.

BEING NEGATIVE IS EXHAUSTING!

Consider embarking on a thoughtful exercise of tracking your daily thoughts over a couple of days—a contemplation of the time spent dwelling on the negative facets of life juxtaposed with moments dedicated to positive reflections. Engaging in such introspection can provide intriguing insights into your mental habits and thought patterns. Surprisingly, even individuals who have reached remarkable levels of accomplishment might find themselves astonished by the significant chunks of time they allocate to negative thinking.

It's truly fascinating that exceptional successes in various realms of the world allocate minimal, if any, time to dwelling on negativity. Instead, they consciously immerse themselves in a sea of positive thoughts and affirmations. These influential figures often attribute their achievements, in part, to their unwavering commitment to focusing solely on the positive aspects of life. Their remarkable journeys underscore the power of positive thinking and the profound influence it can wield over one's life trajectory and success. Allow me to share an enlightening anecdote about Henry Ford, a figure emblematic of boundless achievement. When asked if there was anything he wished for but couldn't achieve, his response was unwavering: he firmly believed there wasn't. Reflecting on his journey, he acknowledged moments when he grappled with the concept of limitations before mastering the art of harnessing his mind. However, Ford's philosophy was nothing short of remarkable—he emphasized the importance of focusing on what he could do rather than fixating on what seemed impossible.

His philosophy encapsulates a profound truth that resonates through the ages—concentrating on actionable aspects rather than fixating on limitations. It's about channeling energy into what's achievable and taking tangible steps, rather than getting entangled in thoughts about the insurmountable. This philosophy serves as a testament to the immense power of directing one's thoughts and efforts toward what's within their control, fostering a mindset oriented toward possibilities rather than constraints. It's a reminder that the transformative force of a positive mindset lies in its ability to steer focus toward what can be done, sparking innovation and paving the way for unparalleled achievements.

When confronted with challenging problems, it's a common tendency for many to immediately focus on the seemingly insurmountable aspects, listing reasons why resolution might seem impossible. Often, these unfavorable aspects take center stage in their thoughts, overshadowing any potential positive elements. However, from my perspective, I hold firm in the belief that every problem, no matter how daunting, harbors elements that can be leveraged positively.

In my extensive experience navigating through various challenges, I struggle to recall encountering a problem entirely devoid of a silver lining. Even if nothing else, the favorable aspect might simply be the assurance that if the problem is solvable, I possess the capability to resolve it. Conversely, if it extends beyond my immediate capacity, I adopt a mindset of acceptance rather than lingering in distress. Yet, when individuals encounter formidable challenges, many tend to spiral into a negative mental state, succumbing to worry and distress.

It's unfortunate that a considerable number of people tend to engage in this negative pattern of thinking, as it often proves counterproductive, leading to stagnation rather than progress. When the mind becomes clouded with negativity, it impedes clear thinking and obstructs the path toward meaningful accomplishments. Encouraging a shift in mindset, to actively seek potential solutions and embrace even the smallest positive aspects within a problem, can fundamentally alter the trajectory of problem-solving and pave the way for innovative solutions and personal growth.

Maintaining a positive mindset in the face of adversity is not just about wishful thinking; it's a powerful tool for navigating life's challenges. A positive mental state goes beyond mere optimism; it's a mindset that fosters clarity, resilience, and a proactive approach to problem-solving. It serves as a catalyst for forward momentum and paves the way for productive actions and innovative solutions. Therefore, the real essence lies in learning to consistently uphold a positive outlook, as it forms the fertile ground where significant achievements take root and flourish.

Consider a positive mental attitude as a magnetic force, drawing in and welcoming opportunities. It operates like a beacon, signaling openness, readiness, and optimism to the world. This creates a conducive environment where opportunities feel not just noticed but genuinely appreciated and welcomed.

Conversely, a negative mental attitude functions as a repellent, a barrier that actively pushes away potential opportunities. When one's mindset is clouded with negativity—whether it's doubt, pessimism, or a sense of incapability—it erects walls that deter opportunities from gravitating towards them. It's as though a force field repels these possibilities, hindering their arrival or even their recognition. Thus, by embracing a positive mindset, individuals not only invite opportunities but also cultivate a mindset conducive to recognizing and capitalizing on them when they arise.

The impact of one's mental outlook on the influx of opportunities is profound. A positive mental attitude not only nurtures receptivity but also fuels the proactive pursuit and identification of opportunities. In contrast, a negative mindset not only obstructs the inflow of opportunities but also limits one's ability to recognize or seize them when they arise. Therefore, nurturing a positive mental attitude is not just about fostering a cheerful disposition but also about actively creating a fertile ground where opportunities are drawn in and welcomed with open arms.

The idea that repelling opportunities is linked to one's merit or entitlement to those opportunities is far from the truth. In reality, your right to the good things in life isn't diminished by your circumstances or your inherent worthiness. However, the presence of a negative mental attitude often acts as a barrier, creating a force that repels potential opportunities that could lead to the attainment of those good things.

Maintaining a positive mindset is not just about putting on a facade of positivity; it's a deliberate effort to create an environment that actively draws in the opportunities aligning with your aspirations and ambitions. By consistently nurturing a positive mental state, you effectively generate a magnetic force that attracts the things you desire and actively pursue in life.

Consider the perplexing phenomenon encountered by many despite fervent prayers: the outcomes often appear disappointing or even contrary to expectations. This puzzling scenario echoes across various faiths and belief systems. Its roots lie in a fundamental law—an unwavering principle that governs the workings of the mind and the nature of reality itself. This universal law operates on the principle that the mind tends to attract reflections of the thoughts it predominantly dwells upon. Remarkably, this law holds true for all individuals, irrespective of their faith or belief system. When the mind is steeped in negativity, it inadvertently draws corresponding negative outcomes or results, influencing even the outcomes of prayers and aspirations.

To alter this pattern and attract the outcomes desired, it's essential to cultivate a positive mental attitude. Belief alone isn't sufficient; it must be accompanied by active steps and transformed into applied faith. However, the coexistence of a negative state of mind and applied faith is impossible—they're inherently incompatible. Therefore, fostering a positive mindset isn't just a notion but a fundamental requirement to align your beliefs, actions, and desires with the outcomes you seek.

Recognizing the profound impact of one's daily surroundings on maintaining a positive mental attitude prompts many individuals to employ uplifting mottoes or affirmations. The R. J. Letourneau Company, housing around two thousand employees, exemplifies this practice by strategically placing prominently printed mottoes throughout its sprawling industrial plant. These mottoes, meticulously chosen for their constructive essence, were strategically displayed across various departments, vividly printed in large half-foot letters for maximum visibility.

Imagine walking into your workplace and encountering a compelling motto displayed across the expanse of the building every single day. This visual reinforcement left an indelible impression on the employees. In the bustling cafeteria, where the workforce congregated for meals, these mottos became a focal point, each carrying its specific message to inspire and remind everyone of their potential and worth.

The incident featuring the motto, "Just remember that your real boss is the one who walks around under your hat," served as a testament not only to the potency but also the delightful nuances in interpreting motivational messages. While the intended meaning was clear, it sparked an unexpected yet clever response from an individual who humorously related it to their foreman. This amusing turn of events not only brought a smile but also offered a subtle insight into the diversity of perceptions such messages can evoke.

This experience sheds light on the multifaceted nature of interpretations and underscores the vital role of consistent exposure to such positive affirmations. The regular presence of these empowering mottos in various workplace settings cultivates an atmosphere that promotes self-empowerment. It reinforces the profound idea that each individual holds the reins to their destiny. The continual exposure to these affirmations nurtures a mindset where individuals recognize their autonomy and take charge of their own paths, instilling a sense of accountability and determination.

STEPS FOR TRANSMUTATION

The process of transforming failure into success, poverty into riches, sorrow into joy, and fear into faith involves a method rooted in cultivating a positive mental attitude. Success, wealth, and faith thrive in the soil of positivity, incapable of flourishing within a negative mindset. This transmutation process, while straightforward, holds immense power. It's a transformative journey that warrants revisiting, internalizing, and truly making a part of oneself.

1. **When confronted with failure, a powerful approach is to reimagine it as a success.** While this might seem challenging initially, it's not an impossible feat. Instead of dwelling on the failure, visualize what might have occurred if it had been a success. Place yourself within the scenario of success rather than viewing yourself from the lens of failure. This shift in perspective involves actively seeking

the positive aspects hidden within the failure—every defeat holds within it the potential for an equivalent benefit. Identifying this seed of opportunity within adversity allows the transmutation of failure into success. The process entails embracing a positive mental attitude, as seeking this seed assures its discovery. It may not manifest immediately, but with persistent pursuit, it's sure to reveal itself.

2. **When poverty looms or has become a reality, it's transformative to envision it as wealth.** Visualizing the richness of life and the endless possibilities that wealth could bring is a powerful exercise. Seeking the equivalent benefit within poverty can be transformative. I recall a moment from my childhood, sitting by a river in Wise County, hungry and without enough food. In that moment of despair, I closed my eyes and envisioned a different future for myself. I saw myself achieving fame and wealth, returning to that very spot on a steam-powered mechanical horse, hearing the click of its horseshoes on the rocks. This visualization, amid poverty and hunger, allowed me to build a mental image of abundance and success, creating a sense of ecstasy and hope amidst the lack and need.

As time elapsed, I found myself driving my cherished Rolls-Royce back to that very spot—a place that once framed my childhood scene of poverty and hunger. Sitting there in the opulent interior of a car that carried a price tag of $22,500, I retraced the steps of my past. I paused and reflected on that moment from my youth, revisiting the vivid imagination I had conjured up in those early days of lack and want. I pondered, wondering if my youthful imagination had any influence on my eventual success. Perhaps, in nurturing that hope amid hardships, I managed to sustain that hope, transforming it gradually into faith.

And over time, that faith didn't just bring me the envisioned steam-powered horse; it unfolded into something far more invaluable and precious.

The key lies in envisioning a future that sparkles with the things you desire. It involves the transmutation of unfavorable circumstances and adversities into mental images that exude pleasure and contentment. This practice requires a conscious shift, redirecting your mind away from dwelling on unpleasant situations and steering it towards envisioning scenarios that radiate positivity and fulfillment.

3. **When fear looms large in your life, recognize that it is essentially faith operating in reverse gear.** It's crucial to shift gears and start viewing situations through the lens of faith. Picture yourself manifesting faith in every circumstance or outcome you desire. It's a universal experience for individuals to grapple with the seven fundamental fears at different junctures in life, often persisting throughout their journey. However, allowing fear to take root and dominate not only solidifies it as a habit but also draws undesirable circumstances towards you. To confront fear effectively, it's imperative to mentally transmute or convert it into its polar opposite—faith. This transformation not only counteracts fear but also attracts positive outcomes and desired circumstances.

   If the fear of poverty creeps in, shift your focus to envisioning opulence and financial prosperity. Explore the ways and strategies you'll employ to earn and attain wealth, considering how you'll utilize it once acquired. There's immense power in daydreaming about the wealth you aspire to amass rather than dwelling on the poverty that currently exists. There's no advantage in lamenting your financial state or worrying about the lack of money without seeking solutions.

In my perspective, there's nothing materialistic that I desire and can't acquire with resources, including money. Instead of fixating on limitations, I cultivate a mindset oriented towards possibilities. This approach has been ingrained in me for a considerable period, emphasizing the significance of conditioning the mind towards positivity. This conditioning serves as a foundation, ensuring a habitual positive response when faced with situations demanding a positive mental outlook.

It's vital to understand that a positive mental attitude isn't attained merely through wishes; it's an incremental process, akin to weaving a rope, each thread added gradually, day by day. Developing a positive mindset is an ongoing journey that evolves steadily, not an immediate transformation that occurs overnight.

HELPFUL INVISIBLE GUIDES

Cultivate within your mind an imaginary legion of invisible guides, entrusted with meeting your every need and fulfilling your desires. It might sound fantastical if you're not acquainted with metaphysical concepts or this philosophy. However, for me, this isn't a whimsical concept; it's a structured system that actively tends to my requirements and wishes. Admittedly, there have been moments when even the guide responsible for my physical well-being seemed a bit lax last week. But I took action—rousing and revitalizing this guide—which resulted in a surge of energy that I've not experienced in a while. Surprisingly, that brief setback served as a reminder to express gratitude to this guide for sound physical health, preventing any further neglect.

While I acknowledge that these guides are products of my

imagination, I'm under no illusion that they are tangible entities. Yet, for practical purposes, they represent tangible forces and individuals. Each guide diligently fulfills the specific role I've assigned, continuously and without fail.

GUIDE FOR PHYSICAL SOUND HEALTH

Nurturing physical well-being stands as the cornerstone of this invisible cadre. Why give it precedence? Consider the synergy between a sharp mind and a robust body. A healthy physique becomes the haven for the intellect—it must operate at peak efficiency, thriving with energy and resilience. Enthusiasm, a vital ingredient, demands an abundant reserve of both physical and mental vitality. Sustaining fervor becomes a challenge when physical discomfort pervades.

Caring for your physical self emerges as a primary responsibility. Ensuring its responsiveness to your demands is pivotal—it's your engine room. Even beyond your conscious efforts in the day, during rest, the natural restorative process unfolds, revitalizing and fine-tuning your body. This endeavor calls for a specialized overseer, the guide to sound health, assigned to supervise this rejuvenation, ensuring it unfolds efficiently. This trained guide remains instrumental in providing the essential attention and upkeep your body requires.

GUIDE TO FINANCIAL PROSPERITY

When it comes to achieving financial prosperity, having the right guide can be pivotal. Consider this: Is there anyone you know who can selflessly serve others without the use of money? While the notion of living without money might seem idealistic, the truth remains that money holds significance. It's about cultivating a consciousness around money, and the guide outlined here plays a crucial role in shaping that mindset.

My guide operates within strict parameters—I don't allow it to solely focus on making money. There's a boundary I've set against greed, an excessive desire for wealth, or overpaying for what's earned. I've witnessed individuals striving so ardently for wealth that they sacrifice their health and happiness. In the end, the surplus wealth often leads to posthumous conflicts among their heirs. That's a fate I'm determined to avoid. My aim is to have enough, striking that balance without crossing into excessive accumulation.

The pursuit of money can become an endless cycle for many. The common narrative often involves statements like, "I'll earn my first million, then retire." Yet, I recall Bing Crosby's declaration to his brother-manager that earning $50,000 would suffice for them to stop. Today, they surpass a million annually and find themselves deeper in the competitive race, toiling harder than before. This isn't a criticism; Bing's someone I respect deeply. I'm addressing the broader pattern of people chasing things they don't truly need, paying an exorbitant price in effort and sometimes health.

Ultimately, it's crucial to strike a balance between financial ambition and contentment. The guide I follow ensures I maintain that equilibrium—enough to thrive without excessive pursuit.

This philosophy centers on achieving economic success without sacrificing your well-being or prematurely shortening your life in pursuit of excessive accumulation. The key? Recognizing when you've reached a point of sufficiency. It's about optimizing the utility of your current possessions rather than relentlessly pursuing more items that won't enhance your life.

Reflecting on a poignant biblical sentiment, it conveys the

essence of moderation: "Not too much, not too little—just enough." This philosophy echoes this sentiment, emphasizing the pursuit of balance in all aspects. Understanding the concept of 'enough' versus 'excessive' is a profound aspect of this philosophy. It bestows the gift of leading a harmonious and balanced life, guiding individuals to discern their personal thresholds of contentment and excess. Discovering that delicate equilibrium between sufficiency and surplus becomes a cherished aspect of this philosophy's teachings.

GUIDE TO PEACE OF MIND

The Importance of Peace of Mind and Balanced Living:

1. **Wealth vs. Peace of Mind:** The pursuit of wealth and material possessions often takes precedence in our endeavors, yet the ultimate measure of success encompasses more than material riches. Even amidst opulence, an absence of inner tranquility can eclipse any sense of accomplishment. The value of peace of mind far exceeds the accumulation of wealth, emphasizing the necessity of finding harmony between external success and internal contentment.
2. **Intimate Insights into Success:** Through intimate interactions with affluent individuals and witnessing their lives from close quarters, a profound revelation emerged—the essence of a balanced life. Observing not just their professional triumphs but the intricate dynamics of their families and the aftermath of their passing illuminated the significance of harmony and equilibrium in life. It underscored that genuine success transcends mere financial prosperity; it embodies a well-

rounded life encompassing family, relationships, health, and purpose.
3. **Balanced Living as a Game:** Life, akin to a game, thrives on the joy found in daily pursuits. Approaching life as a game to be fervently played, relishing every moment, and finding fulfillment in one's daily occupation becomes a cornerstone of maintaining inner peace. This perspective encourages embracing life's challenges and victories with a sense of enthusiasm, fostering a mindset focused on growth and enjoyment in the journey.
4. **Labor of Love:** Society often perpetuates a norm where work is seen as a means of survival rather than an expression of passion. The rarity of individuals engaged in work they genuinely love reflects a societal imbalance. Achieving a state where one can pursue activities out of sheer passion rather than necessity is a rarity and a significant indicator of fortunate circumstances.
5. **The Path to Fulfillment:** This philosophy advocates for aligning actions with love and desire rather than mere obligation. However, achieving this state demands consistent dedication to maintaining a positive mental attitude. It's about cultivating a mindset rooted in positivity, which in turn drives actions fueled by passion and purpose, leading to a more fulfilling existence.

The Unique Insights of Collaborators in Building a Philosophy

In the journey of formulating this philosophy, my collaborators were exemplary figures, representing the pinnacle of success across diverse fields during their time. Each individual stood as a beacon of achievement in their respective domains. Among this esteemed group, only a solitary figure stood out, even remotely embodying a sense of peace alongside their accomplishments: John Burroughs. His proximity to inner tranquility amid success was notable.

Following Burroughs, Mr. Edison emerged as the next closest in attaining a semblance of peace amidst his achievements. Then, Mr. Carnegie holds the third position in this evaluation. However, his later years witnessed a poignant struggle—an almost frantic quest to divest himself of his wealth, striving to distribute it where it could benefit without harm. This endeavor became a consuming obsession, almost unsettling his mental balance. His fervent desire was to shape this philosophy, to ensure it equipped people with the knowledge to acquire material wealth, including money, without infringing upon the rights of others.

In his final years, Mr. Carnegie yearned for the organized dissemination of this philosophy among the populace, longing for it more than anything else in the world. Tragically, his demise in 1919 precluded him from witnessing the translation of these concepts into written form and the creation of the initial books. Until his passing, he meticulously consulted and cross-examined me on fifteen out of the seventeen foundational principles that compose this philosophy. His earnest dedication to ensuring the ethical acquisition of wealth and knowledge remains an integral part of this philosophy's legacy.

Reflecting on pivotal figures in my life, I've often lamented the absence of two individuals during my moments of triumph—the ones who witnessed my struggles and opposition. These significant figures were my stepmother and my mentor, Andrew Carnegie. To have shared my success with them would have been a profound joy and a fitting tribute to their guidance during my times of need. I've often felt a sense of their presence, almost as if they're observing my endeavors even now.

At times, I'm convinced that someone, perhaps these influential figures, watches over my actions. I've noticed instances where my decisions and actions transcend my usual capabilities, especially in recent years. It's as though there's a guiding presence standing beside me, prompting me toward brilliance. During critical moments demanding significant choices, I can almost sense this presence guiding my decisions—an almost tangible influence that feels akin to a physical presence.

Despite my accomplishments being attributed to the collaboration of hundreds of individuals who assisted me, I acknowledge that their collective effort alone wouldn't have sufficed. There's an unspoken factor, an influence beyond the tangible collaboration, that has played a pivotal role in the creation and success of this philosophy. It's an aspect I've refrained from discussing extensively, as I wish not to convey a sense of favoritism or possessiveness over something that others couldn't access or replicate.

My sincere belief stands firm: there isn't anything within my reach that isn't equally accessible to anyone else. The sources of inspiration, motivation, and guidance I draw upon are not exclusive privileges; they are open to all. It's a conviction that resonates deeply within me, a belief I wholeheartedly hold. The wellspring of inspiration I tap into is not a restricted reserve but a boundless reservoir, equally available to each individual seeking it. This belief in the universality of these sources is at the core of my perspective, one that I firmly stand by.

GUIDES OF HOPE AND FAITH

Contemplating hope and faith, I perceive them as inseparable twins—integral guides that navigate life's journey. Consider this: without the perpetual flames of hope and faith flickering within us, what purpose or motivation would propel our existence? They serve as fundamental pillars upon which our aspirations and existence stand.

Yet, to safeguard these essential virtues from the onslaught of external forces—a barrage of circumstances, people, and uncontrollable elements—a robust system is indispensable. It acts as a shield, a resistance against anything that threatens to erode hope and faith. Life unfailingly presents challenges, and countering these requires a structured approach, an antidote that one can wield and rely upon in times of upheaval.

In my experience, I've found solace and strength in eight guiding principles that form the bedrock of my resilience. They have served as a fortress against adversities, consistently reinforcing hope and faith within me. Notably, I've imparted these principles to numerous others, witnessing their efficacy in sustaining hope and faith for others as they have for me. This structured approach, this systematic reinforcement, remains an invaluable asset in nurturing and preserving the flames of hope and faith amid life's unpredictable tides.

GUIDES OF LOVE AND ROMANCE

The duo of love and romance stands as another pair of guiding forces, essential in life's journey. Consider this: infusing any endeavor with a touch of romance is key to its worth and enjoyment. Without this romanticized perspective, activities often lack the zest and joy they could otherwise offer. Love, an intrinsic human emotion, distinguishes us from lower beings—it's our ability to express and experience this emotion that sets us apart. Love, in its essence, is a profound catalyst, shaping geniuses and forging leaders, while also being instrumental in maintaining robust health.

The capacity to love isn't just a sentiment; it's a gateway to rubbing shoulders with genius. Love, coupled with romance, operates as a dual force in my life. They facilitate my alignment with tasks, ensuring that I approach them with warmth and stay youthful in both body and mind. Their influence extends beyond maintaining youthfulness; they infuse my endeavors with an enduring enthusiasm. This perspective transcends the notion of toil; instead, everything becomes an act of passion and devotion. I don't perceive anything as hard work because, in essence, I approach every task as a form of play—a labor of love. This perspective eliminates drudgery and ensures that every task is enveloped in a sense of joy and purpose.

Acknowledging the reality that achieving a state where economic concerns no longer dominate one's existence might initially dim the pleasure found in work. However, there exists a transformative possibility—to cultivate a system that infuses every task with the essence of love and passion, transcending mundane chores into acts of fulfillment. Whether it's washing dishes or engaging in physically demanding tasks like digging ditches, adopting an approach that converts these actions into acts of love becomes paramount.

For instance, when I return home, I willingly assist Annie Lou in washing dishes. Not because she lacks the ability to do so herself, but because I cherish the opportunity to contribute. Engaging in this activity brings me immense joy—it's not about superiority but about embracing the joy of shared tasks. Furthermore, tending to the garden isn't beyond my reach either. In fact, I relish the chance to participate as it not only provides a healthy tan but also fosters good health and a sense of fulfillment. Embracing a simpler life, one that celebrates humanity over pretenses or rigidity, holds significant value. Nobody truly desires to be something impersonal or detached, but rather to revel in being genuine human beings.

The crux lies in embedding love and romance into every facet of life, creating a habitual expression that transcends boundaries. This systematic integration ensures that the inclination towards love and passion naturally infuses itself into every action and task undertaken.

GUIDE FOR OVERALL WISDOM

The paramount guide to overall wisdom presides over the other seven, orchestrating their continuous engagement in serving your life's purpose. Its pivotal role lies in seamlessly aligning you with every circumstance life presents, be it favorable or adverse, ensuring that each experience contributes to your growth. In my journey, I've adopted a perspective where every aspect of life, be it pleasant or challenging, serves as valuable grist for the mill of learning and progress. I diligently transform every encounter into material for growth, grinding even the most unpleasant experiences to extract their wisdom and lessons.

It's an understanding that no experience, whether positive or negative, goes to waste if one adapts oneself to derive its teachings. Every life episode holds potential for personal enrichment when approached with the right mindset and system. However, permitting unchecked emotions to govern and harbor past unpleasant experiences into adulthood can inadvertently attract more negativity into one's life. Yet, the intriguing aspect about adversity is its inherent cowardice. By adopting a proactive stance, welcoming challenging situations as opportunities for growth, one can exert control over them.

It's akin to beckoning these circumstances forth and presenting them with a task, asserting, "Come, join me in this harness; I'll set you to work." Remarkably, when faced with this proactive demeanor, these challenges often recede, seeking occupation elsewhere, and cease frequenting one's path. The key lies in transforming adversity into opportunity, harnessing their potential for personal development, and steering their influence toward constructive pathways.

When one harbors a fear of unpleasant circumstances, it often seems as though these unwelcome experiences arrive in abundance, besieging from every corner—sneaking through backdoors, barging in through front entrances, catching us unawares or unprepared. I don't actively seek out or invite these challenging encounters, but if they happen to find their way into my life, they soon discover that they become mere grist for my life's mill. Undoubtedly, I transform these challenges into valuable material for growth and learning—yet, crucially, I refuse to be overwhelmed by them.

The irony lies in the fact that the more one fears these adversities, the more likely they seem to manifest. They infiltrate our lives unexpectedly, catching us off guard. However, I've adopted a perspective where if these unwelcome circumstances dare to cross my path, they inevitably become a part of the fabric of my life's experiences. I grind them down into lessons, extracting wisdom and insight, but I steadfastly refuse to succumb under their weight.

OBSTACLES TO POSITIVE THINKING

Sustaining a positive mental attitude demands continual vigilance, primarily due to the challenges posed by unpleasant experiences and inherent contradictions that counter positive thinking.

1. **Negative Self's Pursuit of Control:** Within us, there exists a perpetual battle—the negative self persistently seeks dominance. These internal entities tirelessly maneuver to assert control over our psyche, aiming to plunge us into negativity. It's an ongoing vigilance, ensuring these negative influences don't overpower our outlook and steer us away from positivity.
2. **Combatting Accumulated Fears and Limitations:** There's a constant struggle against the accumulation of fears, doubts, and self-imposed restrictions. The task is incessant—addressing these elements continuously to prevent their ascendancy and avoid becoming the predominant force governing our thoughts and actions. Diligent effort is essential to prevent these accumulations from taking hold and shaping our mindset negatively.
3. **Impact of Negative Influences:** External sources, particularly negative individuals, wield significant influence. These negative forces can emanate from close colleagues, cohabitants, and even relatives. The challenge lies in resisting the gravitational pull of their negativity. While it might be unavoidable to coexist with negative individuals, it's crucial not to succumb to their pessimism. It's akin to residing in the same space with negativity without letting it seep into your own mindset. It's an arduous task, yet it's entirely feasible to immunize oneself against such detrimental influences—a feat achieved by remarkable figures like Mahatma Gandhi.
4. **Inherent Negative Traits:** Some negative traits may be ingrained within us from birth. These traits, acquired from the environment we're raised in, can shape our

outlook. For instance, being born into a poverty-stricken environment can instill a deep-seated fear of poverty from an early age. Overcoming these inherent negative traits demands a concerted effort. Ferreting out these traits and transforming them into positive qualities constitutes a significant challenge. I personally encountered and conquered the inborn fear of poverty, stemming from the environment I was born into, which underscores the possibility of transcending these inborn negative tendencies.

5. **Worry Over Financial Stability and Career Progression**: Concerns about financial scarcity or stagnation in one's career path can consume a significant portion of our mental bandwidth. Yet, the choice lies in how we channel this worry—dwelling on the negative aspects or utilizing it as a catalyst for devising solutions. Shifting the focus from worry to constructive problem-solving is pivotal. Persistently dwelling on the negative aspects only serves to entangle us further in an unproductive cycle.

6. **Struggles with Unrequited Love and Emotional Imbalance**: Unreciprocated love or emotional imbalances in relationships can easily upset our emotional equilibrium. However, maintaining a positive mental attitude requires taking charge of one's emotional state. It's essential to prioritize self-balance, steering clear of allowing external emotional turbulence to disrupt our inner peace. It's about recognizing our responsibility to safeguard our mental balance and not permitting others to disrupt it, aligning with the Creator's intention for emotional equilibrium.

7. **Concerns about Health, Real or Perceived**:

Preoccupations about health, whether real or imagined, can be a significant source of worry. These worries can lead to hypochondria, where imagined health concerns take precedence. Addressing these concerns involves managing the anxiety around potential health issues without allowing them to overshadow our lives. Often, fretting about health issues that may never materialize only amplifies our anxieties.

8. **Intolerance and Closed-Mindedness**: Intolerance and a closed mind often obstruct one's path to maintaining a positive mental attitude. These traits hinder acceptance and receptivity to diverse perspectives, creating inner turmoil and fostering a negative outlook.

9. **Greed for Excessive Material Possessions**: The insatiable desire for excessive material wealth can be a significant hurdle in cultivating a positive mental attitude. It involves the struggle of managing the price one pays for accumulation and the conquest of possessions, potentially overshadowing the pursuit of a positive mindset.

10. **Lack of a Defined Life Purpose**: Another critical challenge is navigating life without a clearly defined major purpose. Absence of such clarity can lead to feelings of aimlessness and confusion, hindering the cultivation of a positive mental attitude.

11. **Absence of a Guiding Life Philosophy**: Surprisingly, a significant portion of individuals lack a guiding philosophy for life. Without a foundational philosophy, they navigate existence haphazardly, at the mercy of circumstance and chance. It's akin to being adrift, devoid of a set of guiding principles. To counter this, one needs a robust philosophy to navigate life's

challenges. It's not merely about having a philosophy to die by but, more crucially, one to live by—a guiding set of principles that shapes daily choices and actions.
12. **Dependency on Others' Thoughts**: Allowing others to shape and control our thoughts is a significant impediment to fostering a positive mental attitude. When individuals cede their thinking to external influences, they forfeit their ability to form independent perspectives. This reliance on external thinking inhibits the development of one's own mental fortitude and inhibits the cultivation of a positive mindset.

To truly embrace a positive mental attitude, it's imperative to exercise autonomy in thinking, to cultivate one's unique perspective, and to resist the inclination to outsource one's cognitive processes to external sources. By reclaiming ownership of our thoughts and beliefs, we lay the foundation for a resilient and positive mental outlook.

Embracing this philosophy isn't just about personal fulfillment—it extends far beyond, shaping how you interact and resonate with those around you.

This philosophy offers a pathway to live in a manner that endears you to your neighbors, making you a beacon of positivity and desirability in your community. It's about fostering an environment where both you and those around you find joy and contentment in each other's presence. Not only does it pave the way for personal prosperity, contentment, and peace of mind, but it also radiates these positive qualities to everyone you encounter.

Living by this philosophy isn't merely a personal pursuit; it's an ethos that transcends the individual. It advocates for a mental attitude that cultivates harmony, joy, and a sense of communal well-being. This approach to life isn't just something for personal benefit—it's a template for fostering an environment where everyone can thrive, fostering a collective mindset that resonates positivity and contentment to all who come into contact with it.

TWELVE GREAT AND ENDURING RICHES

Understanding the concept of true and lasting wealth is essential, as it transcends mere financial accumulation. While many aspire to be affluent, the definition of enduring richness comprises twelve distinct facets. Familiarizing oneself with these facets is pivotal, as achieving true wealth necessitates a harmonious amalgamation of these twelve great and enduring riches.

It's intriguing to note the positioning of money within this spectrum. Despite its commonly perceived significance, money holds the twelfth position in this hierarchy. This deliberate placement is a testament to the fact that there exist eleven other invaluable facets that surpass the importance of monetary wealth in crafting a holistic and well-balanced life.

The emphasis lies in acknowledging the significance of these other eleven riches, which take precedence over monetary wealth when it comes to nurturing a well-rounded and fulfilling life. This hierarchy underscores the intricate nature of true richness, highlighting that while financial wealth holds significance, its value pales in comparison to the multifaceted aspects that constitute enduring and comprehensive richness.

6

TRANSCENDING DIFFICULTIES AND PERPLEXITIES

James Allen

"And Perplexities—Man who man would be Must rule the empire of himself; in it Must be supreme, establishing his throne On vanquished will, quelling the anarchy Of hopes and fears, being himself alone."

—Shelley

"Have you missed in your aim? Well, the mark is still shining. Did you faint in the race? Well, take breath for the next.

—Ella Wheelar Wilcose

The notion that within the labyrinth of trials and tribulations nestles a kernel of divine favor might initially strike many as an absurdity. Yet, it's within these enigmatic paradoxes that truth, often elusive, finds its dwelling—a place where the burdens deemed insurmountable by the uninitiated transform into conquests revered by the discerning. Adversities emerge from the abyss of ignorance and vulnerability, beckoning not despair but rather the pursuit of enlightenment and the fortification of one's inner citadel of resilience.

As an individual traverses the path of virtuous existence, the intricate tapestry of challenges slowly begins to unfurl, dissipating like wisps of transient mist in the radiant presence of dawn. Grasp this truth: the nucleus of your trial doesn't merely nest within the external circumstances that birthed it; rather, it festers within the cognitive lens through which you appraise and confront the situation. What may loom as an insurmountable obstacle to a child presents itself as a mere stepping stone to the sagacious mind of an adult. Equally so, what clouds the intellect of the unenlightened in bewildering perplexity would hardly stir a ripple in the sea of understanding for the discerning.

Reflect upon the naive mind of a child—how colossal and seemingly insurmountable the hurdles appear in the pursuit of even the most rudimentary lessons. Countless moments, fraught with anxiety, stretch into hours, days, and at times, even months, spent in unraveling the labyrinthine mysteries, often accompanied by tears shed in anguish at the sight of an unconquered, seemingly impregnable bastion of adversity. Yet, acknowledge this: the challenge primarily resides in the child's nascent comprehension, and its conquest and resolution serve as an indispensable crucible, tempering the blade of intellect and laying the cornerstone toward the eventual edifice of wisdom, happiness, and the indispensable utility of the child's burgeoning potential.

Similarly, such is the nature of the tribulations that weave through the tapestry of older children's lives, compelling them, for the very sake of their personal evolution and maturation, to decipher and conquer. Each conquered obstacle signifies not only an accumulation of experience but also a profound insight gained, and wisdom earned—a vital lesson etched into the fabric of their being, accompanied by the jubilant liberation that comes from the triumphant completion of a task.

But what truly defines a difficulty? Is it not a circumstance not yet comprehended in its entirety, its implications not fully grasped? It stands as a beckoning call for the cultivation and exercise of a deeper insight and a broader intellect than previously engaged. It serves as an urgent mandate, summoning forth dormant energies and beseeching the expression and utilization of concealed reservoirs of strength. Thus, disguised beneath its formidable facade, it assumes the guise of a benevolent angel—an ally, a mentor. When approached with serenity and comprehended rightly, it becomes the compass that navigates toward greater contentment and loftier enlightenment.

Imagine a world devoid of difficulties—a realm where progress finds no foothold, growth remains stifled, and evolution ceases to unfurl. In such a stagnant existence, humanity would languish and wither away under the weight of ennui. Hence, let it be proclaimed: rejoice in the face of obstacles, for they signify the terminus of indifference or folly along a specific path, beckoning one to muster every ounce of vigor and intellect to disentangle oneself and pave a superior way forward. These challenges signify an inner outcry for greater liberty, for an expanded arena wherein dormant potentials seek liberation and expression.

The inherent difficulty within any situation seldom originates from the situation itself; rather, it burgeons from the dearth of profound insight into its multifaceted layers and the inadequacy of wisdom in navigating its complexities. Hence, the conquest of a difficulty represents an immeasurable gain—an ascent to higher understanding and a triumph of sagacity.

It's imperative to acknowledge that difficulties aren't haphazardly birthed into existence; they don't emerge capriciously or by happenstance. Instead, they stem from underlying causes, summoned forth by the inexorable law of evolution itself—the unfolding necessities of an individual's existence. And within this emergence lies their inherent benediction—their capacity to foster growth and propel one forward on the path of personal evolution and enlightenment:

1. **Conduct's Impact:** Certain modes of behavior inevitably lead to intricate complications, while others navigate smoothly out of troublesome entanglements. Regardless of how ensnared one feels, there's always a route to liberation.
2. **Self-Liberation:** No matter how deeply one may find themselves embroiled in troubles or lost in bewildering complexities, there's always a way to retrace steps, rediscover simplicity, and rejoin the path to wise and blessed actions.
3. **Response to Dilemma:** Bemoaning, despairing, or aimlessly wishing for a different situation won't resolve the dilemma. Instead, it demands alertness, logical thinking, and composed calculation.
4. **Self-Command:** To overcome difficulties, one must muster self-control, engage in thoughtful introspection, and embark on vigorous efforts to regain equilibrium.
5. **Detriment of Worry:** Anxiety and worry only exacerbate the situation, magnifying the problem's magnitude. Quiet introspection, however, reveals past missteps and provides invaluable lessons.
6. **Reflection and Wisdom:** By retracing one's past actions, acknowledging errors, and discerning alternative, wiser paths, an individual gains a wealth of wisdom, diminishing the overwhelming nature of the difficulty.
7. **Dispassionate Analysis:** By dissecting the difficulty

impartially, understanding its nuances, and comprehending its roots within oneself, the solution begins to emerge clearly.
8. **Permanent Lessons:** The process not only resolves the immediate difficulty but also bestows enduring wisdom and blessedness, becoming an invaluable lesson for the future.

Just as the world presents paths veiled in ignorance, selfishness, folly, and blindness, pathways that invariably lead to confusion and perplexity, so too exist avenues illuminated by knowledge, self-denial, wisdom, and insight, leading toward pleasant and peaceful consummations. One who comprehends this truth approaches difficulties with a courageous spirit, recognizing that in their conquest lies the genesis of truth from error, bliss from pain, and peace from perturbation.

No individual encounters a difficulty that surpasses their capacity to confront and overcome. Worry, far from being merely futile, embodies folly, as it undermines the inherent power and intelligence that are otherwise capable of meeting any challenge. Indeed, every obstacle can be surmounted when approached correctly; hence, anxiety serves no purpose. Furthermore, a challenge that proves insurmountable ceases to be a difficulty and transforms into an impossibility. Even then, anxiety remains unnecessary, for in the face of impossibility, there exists only one course—acceptance. Embracing the inevitable ultimately stands as the most prudent approach.

"Heartily know,
When half-gods go,
The gods arrive."

In the intricate tapestry of existence, much like how domestic, social, and economic quandaries sprout from the seeds of ignorance, blossoming eventually into richer knowledge, so too does every flicker of religious uncertainty, each bout of mental perplexity, and every shadow that obscures the heart herald a forthcoming spiritual ascension. These moments, while clouded in doubt, act as heralds of a brighter intelligence, portending a dawn of greater understanding for those upon whom they cast their enigmatic shroud.

A significant juncture in a person's journey, often unrecognized in the moment, is when bewildering complexities about the enigma of life take root in their consciousness. This juncture signifies the closure of an era defined by apathetic indifference, by the slumber of base instincts, and by the pursuit of mere superficial contentment. Henceforth, the individual begins to exist as an aspiring, self-evolving entity. Transcending the confines of a mere human animal, they embark upon the path of true humanity, dedicating their mental faculties to unraveling life's enigmas and addressing the haunting perplexities that stand as vigilant guardians of truth. These enigmatic challenges stand sentinel at the gate and threshold of the revered Temple of Wisdom, beckoning the seeker to delve deeper into the profound mysteries of existence.

> *"He it is who, when great trials come,*
> *Nor seeks nor shuns them, but doth calmly stay."*

Henceforth, he shall never recline in the cradle of selfish ease or surrender to the seductive embrace of ignorant inertia. No longer will he contentedly gorge on the meager sustenance of fleshly pleasures akin to the swine's husks. There exists no sanctuary for him to escape the persistent murmurs of his heart, echoing its unending, enigmatic inquiries. The divine essence dormant within him has stirred from its slumber; a deity once dormant now sheds the veils of incoherent night visions, refusing to retreat into the oblivion of slumber, resolute in its quest until it basks in the radiant, unobscured daylight of Truth.

For such a transformed soul, the clamor for loftier pursuits and grander accomplishments becomes an incessant chorus, impossible to mute for any extended duration. The faculties of his awakened being shall unceasingly impel him towards the unraveling of his enigmas; therein lies his peace, not in the shadows of transgression, nor in the repose of fallacy, but solely in the embrace of Wisdom. Within this pursuit, he finds solace, the ultimate refuge from the storms of uncertainty and the sanctuary where his restless spirit finally finds respite.

The pinnacle of blessedness awaits the individual who, cognizant of the very ignorance that births their doubts and perplexities, embraces that awareness rather than seeking to conceal it. With earnest resolve, he dedicates himself fervently to its dissolution, tirelessly seeking day after day for the path illuminated by light. This journey leads toward dispelling the encompassing shadows, unravelling doubts, and unraveling the solutions to the pressing dilemmas that besiege his existence. Much like a child rejoices upon mastering a long-persisting lesson, so too does a man's heart find solace and liberty upon satisfactorily overcoming a worldly quandary. Yet, to a far greater magnitude, the heart of an individual is rendered joyous and serene when a profound, everlasting query, pondered over and grappled with for ages, is finally resolved, banishing its obscurity for all eternity.

Refuse to perceive your difficulties and enigmas as omens of impending doom, for by adopting such a perspective, you unwittingly bestow upon them the power of ill portents. Instead, recognize their prophetic nature—harbingers of imminent good, for indeed, they embody such potential. Resist the temptation to evade these challenges, for evasion is futile. Neither attempt to flee from them, as wherever you roam, they shall steadfastly accompany you. Confront them calmly and valiantly; face them with the dispassion and dignity inherent in your being. Assess their dimensions, scrutinize their facets, gauge their potency, and comprehend their essence. Engage with them wholeheartedly, launching an assault that culminates in their eventual defeat. Through this relentless engagement, you will forge an indomitable strength and sharpen your intelligence. In doing so, you shall tread the concealed pathways of blessedness, pathways hidden from the superficial glance, where true growth and enlightenment lie in wait.

> *"This to me is life;*
> *That if life be a burden, I will join*
> *To make it but the burden of a song."*
>
> —Bailey

> *"Have you heard that it was good to gain the day?*
> *I also say it is good to fall, battles are lost in the same*
> *spirit in which they are won."*
>
> —Walt Whitman

7

WILL YOU MASTER MONEY? OR WILL IT MASTER YOU?

Napoleon Hill

Nothing rivals the tranquility of mind, for it stands as life's supreme treasure. A peace of mind can be snatched away by the relentless pursuit of wealth, whether through an anxious scramble for money or through an insatiable quest for more riches than one can judiciously utilize. The earnings derived from purposeful and constructive endeavors tend to yield the most beneficial results. Therein lies the folly of depriving the youth of the indispensable lesson learned through labor.

The true value of money becomes palpable through dedicated efforts to save a portion of one's income. Such practices not only grant a deeper understanding of the worth of monetary resources but also prepare individuals to grasp and seize numerous opportunities that might otherwise slip through their fingers.

In my interactions with young minds, a genuine appreciation for money is often lacking, particularly when the prospect of substantial earnings lies on the distant horizon. Understandably so, for the absence of financial stability can cast a shadow over the very essence of living, threatening to erode the peace of mind.

Thus, the young aspirant sets out on the pursuit of wealth. Initially, spending equals earnings, especially if family plays a part in utilizing the income. However, a successful individual soon reaches a juncture where surplus income emerges, beyond immediate necessities and household expenses. This surplus often finds its way into investments, real estate, and other avenues.

For the individual fostering a positive mindset, this journey transcends mere material accumulation. Gradually, he amasses significant property and wealth, crossing an imperceptible threshold. He becomes 'rich,' not solely in financial terms but in the tranquility that transcends monetary wealth. Such a person, with a considerable surplus above his material needs, stands capable of fulfilling reasonable desires. Consequently, while financial records may declare his affluence, his private ledger should bear witness to the wealth of peace reigning within.

The attainment of peace of mind hinges upon the mastery of money. Should one wield command over their finances, peace becomes an attainable virtue. Conversely, should money reign supreme over the individual, serenity remains elusive, veiled behind the shadows of fiscal dominance.

Often, the ostentatious display of material wealth symbolizes a quest for recognition—a grandiose spectacle meant to garner attention. Reflecting on my own past, I openly acknowledge a penchant for such displays during the days of my Catskill estate. Yet, fortuitously, circumstances led to its loss before it could inflict permanent harm upon my being. Not every individual risks harm by parading their wealth; some seem invigorated by it. However, there exist those who plunge so deeply into conspicuous exhibition that their very essence becomes submerged in a sea of dollars—an indication that they have lost themselves in the spectacle.

Consider the tale of a man who amassed millions only to face sudden bankruptcy. Amidst the wreckage of his financial downfall, legal inquiries unearthed a warehouse brimming with priceless antiquities and magnificent artwork—all purchased with cash. Yet, a startling revelation emerged; most of these treasures lay untouched, unpacked relics that never granted their owner any joy. He delighted in discussing his possessions, painting himself as a modern-day Croesus, but the essence of genuine enjoyment eluded him. This relentless pursuit of accumulation stands in stark contrast to a mind anchored in peace.

The compulsion to accumulate without deriving fulfillment from these possessions resides at the antipode of tranquility. A mind consumed by the acquisition of material possessions resides far from the realm of peace.

The dread of losing one's possessions or descending into poverty often harbors an equally ominous counterpart within the hearts of the affluent—the incessant fear of losing their amassed wealth, or the paranoia that regulations might curtail their capacity to amass fortunes beyond any practical measure.

Allow me to recount an encounter with a majority shareholder of the illustrious Coca-Cola Company, a man whose coffers overflowed with a wealth approximating twenty-five million dollars. Did this accumulation translate into tranquility of mind? Regrettably not. Instead, his mind simmered with animosity and suspicion, predominantly directed at the government. Despite being well into his eighties, his pessimistic foresight prophesied a destitute end orchestrated by governmental interference.

During our last encounter, he posed a poignant query, seeking advice on preserving both his peace of mind and wealth. While I vowed never to engage in a dispute with him for the sake of my own serenity, I held firm to the principle of offering direct responses to direct inquiries. When prompted, I advocated a radical approach: divesting all wealth into United States Savings Bonds for the greater good and symbolically releasing his ties to wealth by incinerating these bonds. My sincere counsel, met with disdain, was dismissed as facetiousness. Yet, I remained resolute in my earnestness, emphasizing that liberation from the shackles of wealth-induced unhappiness could manifest through this symbolic act of release.

Unsurprisingly, my advice fell on deaf ears. Until his final days, he remained ensnared by fear and resentment. I firmly believe that the afflictions plaguing him, pre-dating his demise, were deeply rooted in his affection—not for humanity, but for material wealth. Despite the potential for liberation, he clung steadfastly to the chains of his riches, foregoing peace of mind in favor of an inexorable grasp on financial abundance.

PEACE OVER POWER

Rare indeed are the instances where advising someone to burn their wealth would constitute wise counsel. Yet, the underlying principle holds true for all of us—a truth that transcends riches. There exists nothing, absolutely nothing, more invaluable than the tranquility of your mind. Regrettably, this wisdom often eludes the younger generation; however, some acquire this insight as their life's tapestry unfolds. Yet, there are those who, despite the passage of time, never grasp this truth. It bears repeating: the wealth of peace of mind surpasses all other treasures.

Allow me to clarify that my intent was not to assess the validity of my friend's grievances against the government; indeed, there might have been justifiable aspects to his complaints. Instead, I aimed to highlight his mindset—an attitude steeped in fear and mistrust. This attitude persisted despite his staggering wealth, which exceeded twenty-fivefold the typical millionaire's fortune, presenting ample opportunities to foster happiness for himself and others.

Consider the ponderings of Andrew Carnegie, a luminary in the realm of wealth accumulation. In his later years, his ardent desire was to impart the knowledge of wealth creation to the common person. He belonged to a cadre of enlightened industrialists who recognized the pivotal significance of equitable wealth distribution within a nation.

Carnegie comprehended that richness isn't solely confined to possessing vast fortunes; it encompasses having an abundance. However, he also acknowledged that in the natural course of events, the possession of millions would forever remain an exception. He discerned that fixating on accumulating 'millions' or even 'a million' was an unsuitable pursuit for the majority. Such aspirations often strain individuals, detracting from their peace of mind and, in some cases, resulting in the forfeiture of essentials essential to their well-being.

Repeatedly, Carnegie emphasized the importance of elucidating this understanding—an understanding he sought to instill in me, and one which I have endeavored to disseminate to the best of my ability.

The inquiry into the precise monetary requirement for a fulfilled life prompts a contemplation: How much wealth suffices?

The answer lies in securing a measure of financial stability that ensures comfort and security for oneself and loved ones, coupled with a degree of opulence that imbues life with moments of indulgence and luxury. Pursuing this balance while safeguarding one's peace of mind lays the groundwork for the cultivation of self-assured faith. Surprisingly, from this equilibrium often sprouts an unforeseen capacity for generating wealth beyond initial aspirations. For individuals fostering such an equilibrium, surplus wealth ceases to be a burden; instead, it becomes a tool for broadening horizons and enhancing life experiences. Their ethical compass guides them; having never resorted to deceit or exploitation, they are adept at extending assistance and support to others.

Consider the earnest aspirations of a student from India who traveled extensively to seek counsel. In his correspondence, he ardently professed his life's ambition: to amass wealth exceeding a hundredfold of Henry Ford's accumulations—an astronomical figure of approximately a hundred billion dollars. He envisioned himself as a magnate a hundred thousand times over.

In our ensuing conversation, I probed deeper, questioning his intentions regarding such an exorbitant sum. The implication was clear: what meaningful use could be derived from such a staggering wealth? The essence of this inquiry rests not merely in the attainment of wealth but in the conscious utilization of resources for meaningful ends.

Upon our discussion, the aspiring magnate hesitated before conceding, "Honestly, I don't know." It became evident that the possession of such an astronomical sum by a single individual could potentially wield a destabilizing influence on the world order. However, I redirected the conversation, proposing an alternate perspective: utilizing this wealth to emancipate the people of India from antiquated customs and superstitions. Yet, it became clear that his aspiration primarily revolved around surpassing Henry Ford rather than any profound philanthropic goal.

Delving deeper into self-reflection and employing the principles of the Science of Personal Achievement, he recognized that his ambition had spiraled beyond control. The power of the mind to manifest in reality is potent, but it necessitates a balanced and harmonized mental state. As we navigated through his aspirations, he gradually realized that his true desires could be met with a fraction of the envisioned wealth. This revelation provided much-needed relief to the once-anxious businessman, an importer, who finally experienced a sense of ease.

Interestingly, the narrative didn't conclude there. What some might dismiss as mere coincidence, I perceive as consequential occurrences. Before his return to India, I assisted him in securing multiple contracts for the sale of American-made goods in his homeland. Eventually, his profits accrued to just a little over a quarter of a million dollars—a serendipitous alignment between his revised aspirations and the manifested reality.

The most valuable wealth often stems from labor that directly benefits the individual. As discussed earlier, the process of ensuring that one's assets and property are directed to chosen recipients upon one's demise stands in contrast to the uncontrollable event of death itself.

As you embark on your journey to amass wealth, it's crucial to exercise caution, ensuring that any inheritance you bestow does not inadvertently strip the recipient of their peace of mind. A commonly observed phenomenon suggests that the sons of affluent individuals might not exhibit the same acumen and capabilities as their fathers. This disparity often emerges because the 'old man' earned his wealth through dedicated labor. His financial success paralleled the development of his insights, abilities, and deep understanding of both people and the world. He didn't inherit wealth from his father; rather, he garnered it through his own toil and dedication.

Now, consider the son's perspective. Surrounded by affluence throughout his life, he's cognizant of the impending inheritance of substantial wealth. Even if he possesses an inherent inclination to work diligently, the certainty of future affluence can corrode that inclination. In numerous instances, it's replaced by an inclination to seek unearned gains, denying him one of life's fundamental lessons.

Regardless of whether one inherits vast or modest fortunes, their true value lies in their utilization for the betterment of others. Yet, a father does no favor to his son by depriving him of the necessity to take initiative. Similarly, a testator does no favor to the beneficiary by eliminating the need for them to engage in work. While it's commendable to shield inheritors from the harshness of poverty, it's essential not to shelter them from life's realities by surrounding them with an impenetrable wall of wealth. Grant them the priceless opportunity to forge better lives through the wisdom acquired from life's experiences and their own diligent efforts.

During my youthful years, I found myself employed as a secretary to a prosperous lawyer who had two sons older than myself. These young men pursued their education at the esteemed University of Virginia. It fell upon me to issue each of them a monthly check of one hundred dollars as discretionary spending money—a sum that in those times held a purchasing power three or four times greater than its current equivalent. Oh, how I yearned for the privilege they enjoyed!

Reflecting on my own past experiences attending business college, where my primary focus was acquiring the skills necessary to earn a livelihood, I vividly recollect moments of genuine hunger due to the absence of even a penny in my pocket. I distinctly remember standing outside a store, eyeing a bunch of apples priced at six for a dime, my mouth watering at the thought. Eventually, I summoned the courage to negotiate with the storekeeper, persuading him to trust me for the dime until I completed my education and commenced earning my own income. Such memories flooded my thoughts as I penned those enviable monthly checks.

Time rolled by, and my employer's sons returned home adorned with their academic achievements. However, alongside their degrees came a predilection for a life of comfort, with little comprehension of the essence of hard work. Were they inherently as capable as their father? The question remains unanswered. One son secured a prestigious position in a bank owned by his father, while the other assumed managerial responsibilities at a coal mine owned by the family.

A decade hence, a tragic turn of events transpired: they had not only squandered their father's fortune but also deteriorated his health in the process. Their lack of understanding regarding the value of hard work and financial responsibility culminated in the wreckage of their father's legacy and well-being.

Envy, I've learned, has no place in nurturing a peaceful state of mind. Looking back, I find a sense of gratitude for the trials I encountered, including the humbling experience of negotiating a ten-cent long-term credit. Those moments, as arduous as they were, instilled in me a resilience and resourcefulness that later became invaluable. Moreover, as I reflect on my journey towards financial independence, I'm appreciative that my capacity to earn money became intertwined with my personal fulfillment.

Mistakes and financial losses, though painful, held profound lessons. Having no affluent father to cushion the blows of my errors, I encountered adversity as a formidable instructor. It was through these trials that I unearthed resilience and wisdom, forging a path toward personal growth and understanding.

My book, "Think and Grow Rich," has reached the hands of approximately seven million individuals. Over the past two decades since its publication, I've had the privilege of engaging with some of these readers. It's heartening to witness that for some, the book has been a guiding light, assisting them not just in amassing monetary wealth but in achieving a holistic richness in life. However, it's equally apparent that for others, the book primarily became a tool for amassing financial riches alone.

This divergence in interpretation reinforces the idea that the pursuit of wealth, while crucial, should not overshadow the quest for holistic enrichment encompassing personal growth, fulfillment, and contribution to others. Money, though a vital aspect of life, shouldn't be the singular pursuit; rather, it should align with a broader vision of fulfillment and prosperity across all facets of one's being.

THE TWELVE GREAT RICHES OF LIFE

1. A positive mental attitude
2. Sound physical health
3. Harmony in human relationships
4. Freedom from all forms of fear
5. The hope of future achievement
6. The capacity for faith
7. A willingness to share one's blessings
8. A labor of love as an occupation
9. An open mind on all subjects
10. Self-discipline in all circumstances
11. The capacity to understand others
12. Sufficient money

The treasures that truly enrich life should walk hand in hand with the tranquility of mind. It's noteworthy how I've deliberately positioned money at the bottom of this hierarchy, despite persistently asserting its importance in securing peace of mind. I've chosen this sequence because inherently, your own focus leans towards the significance of monetary wealth. However, I must intermittently stress the need to de-prioritize money. It's essential to remember that while money can facilitate numerous things, it cannot directly purchase peace of mind; it merely assists in its pursuit. The true journey to finding peace begins within oneself, irrespective of external circumstances.

In outlining fundamental principles for enhancing income, there's a prevalent notion suggesting it's illogical to caution individuals about the misuse of money, especially when they might not possess enough of it to warrant such concerns. While this advice seems logical, if I were solely writing a book on the art of earning money, this book endeavors to be more. It's not just about acquiring wealth; it's about providing a compass for understanding one's direction and cultivating the right mindset from the outset.

This book aspires to equip you not only with strategies for income generation but also with a vision of your destination and how the world appears once you arrive. Its intent lies in nurturing the correct attitudes and perspectives right from the inception of your financial journey.

While we've emphasized the importance of fostering these critical attitudes, I'd like to delve into practical strategies that individuals with limited or no capital can employ to commence their journey towards wealth creation. Each strategy holds its unique identity yet possesses the potential for infinite customization. As you peruse these methods, I urge you to pause and introspect, aligning these approaches with your personal strengths, the environment you inhabit, and, most importantly, your aspirations.

1. Collaborate with others to bolster their businesses while enhancing your own. Let me illustrate with an anecdote: a young life insurance salesman grappled with difficulties in selling policies to household heads. However, he

transformed this challenge into an opportunity by contemplating a shift in approach. Instead of targeting these individuals in their familial roles, he explored the prospect of selling insurance to them in their capacity as businessmen. Why? Because funds withdrawn from a family's budget represent an immediate loss, whereas an expenditure for business purposes presents the prospect of generating multiple returns.

Consider this: money channeled into business expenses has the potential to yield exponential gains. Therefore, aligning your services or products to aid other businesses not only supports their growth but also offers a pathway to multiply your returns. This strategic shift in perspective can be a pivotal starting point for those seeking to build their wealth from scratch.

This enterprising insurance salesman embarked on an innovative approach to forge partnerships with local businesses. His initial endeavor commenced with a prominent restaurant owner in his town. Recognizing the potential symbiosis between insurance and the hospitality industry, he proposed an ingenious marketing strategy. He suggested that the restaurateur could leverage the quality of his food as not only delicious but also health-promoting, potentially leading to a longer lifespan for patrons. Embracing this concept, the restaurant owner vowed to maintain the high standards and health benefits of his offerings. Building upon this foundation, the insurance agent elucidated the broader plan. The restaurant owner would extend an offer to insure the lives of regular customers for a thousand dollars each. Collaboratively, they hashed out the specifics, and the proposal significantly elevated the restaurant's business. Undoubtedly, this innovative approach also bolstered the insurance agent's burgeoning career.

Expanding his inventive strategy, the salesman applied a similar concept to a consortium of filling stations, a large grocery store, and various other enterprises. While the attribution of originating the concept of appending life insurance to mortgages remains uncertain, this proactive salesman astutely recognized and effectively utilized this angle as part of his repertoire. Leveraging this strategy not only enhanced the financial prospects of these businesses but also fortified his position in the insurance industry, solidifying his reputation as an astute and innovative agent.

Consider this: How can you transform others' support for their businesses into an asset for your own endeavors?

2. Enlighten individuals on maximizing their investments. This isn't about positioning yourself as a business consultant, awaiting people to seek advice on optimizing their spending. Rather, it involves taking the proactive stance of offering insights to others.

Allow me to illustrate with a compelling example: A diligent worker employed at a magazine distributor, earning a modest wage, keenly observed the diverse forms of printing utilized. Similar to a previously mentioned individual, he discerned that many printing tasks lacked finesse and sophistication.

Intriguingly, he realized a fundamental truth: most tasks across industries fall short of their optimal execution. This insight is crucial, as it harbors immense potential for prosperity.

Motivated by this revelation, the young man delved deeper into the nuances of printing and subsequently approached a prominent printing firm. Negotiating a deal for a 10 percent commission, he initiated a partnership to channel printing jobs to the firm. To fortify his expertise, he diligently amassed a plethora of printed material samples from significant users in the industry, meticulously studying them at home.

This initiative exemplifies a proactive approach toward enlightening others about optimization opportunities while simultaneously forging partnerships that benefit all parties involved. It's a testament to the transformative power of insight and proactive engagement within one's industry.

The young man, recognizing the potential for enhancement in various brochures, took a strategic approach. He engaged a freelance commercial artist and an advertising copywriter to develop sample layouts, under a fair compensation agreement if the work materialized. Armed with improved prototypes, he presented these to the respective firms, showcasing how the brochures could be significantly enhanced.

Now, let's delve into the underlying psychological dynamics at play here:

Firstly, many individuals or companies may persist indefinitely with processes or products that merely "get by." Oftentimes, they might not even recognize the need for improvement, or if they do, they might lack the motivation or initiative to address it.

However, when someone enters the picture and not only evokes dissatisfaction with the status quo but simultaneously provides a solution, it's a game-changer. This individual not only instills a sense of discontentment but also offers a tangible pathway to improvement, alleviating the need for additional effort on the part of the recipient. It becomes a compelling proposition: Why wouldn't one take advantage of such an opportunity?

Now, consider this for your own endeavors: How can you effectively demonstrate to others how they can optimize their investments or processes? Further, how can you provide value in a manner that makes them reliant on your expertise repeatedly?

It's about not only offering a solution but establishing yourself as a consistent resource, fostering a dependency on your knowledge and guidance for continued improvement.

3. The evolution of transportation, especially with the advent of automobiles, revolutionized the way farmers brought their goods to market. In the past, a farmer's journey to town, often through challenging terrains on muddy roads with horse-drawn wagons, was an arduous task. Despite the difficulties, they persevered to sell their produce.

As the automobile gained prominence, significant improvements in road infrastructure followed suit. This transformation allowed farmers to transport their goods over greater distances within the same day. The increased mobility paved the way for the establishment of marketing centers strategically positioned between towns. These centers capitalized on the burgeoning car traffic, becoming crucial hubs for farmers to supply their produce and for consumers to access fresh goods conveniently.

Reflecting on the historical dynamics, farmers previously relied on occasional visits from peddlers, who traversed long distances, sometimes on foot with hefty packs. These peddlers were more than merchants; they served as conduits for vital commodities like needles, tobacco, fish hooks, and, notably, news. News was a precious commodity back then, eagerly awaited by rural households. These peddlers, often possessing more financial resources than farmers, acted as critical intermediaries, bridging the gap between producer and consumer.

Moreover, in transactions such as buying or selling horses, brokers played a pivotal role. Their expertise assisted both parties in reaching agreeable terms, often sealing deals with a handshake. These brokers, profiting from their role as mediators between producers and consumers, significantly augmented their financial standing.

The historical context reveals the pivotal role intermediaries played in connecting producers with consumers, accentuating the significance of these linkages in economic transactions.

In recent times, reports have surfaced regarding the grievances of shoppers within the Soviet Union, where individuals spend extensive hours queuing up in front of various specialized food stores. However, it's intriguing to note that these inconveniences might pave the way for the adoption of a more efficient shopping model—akin to the American concept of supermarkets. The shift toward convenient supermarkets, aggregating numerous producers and consumers under one roof, has not only streamlined shopping experiences but has also marked a revolution in merchandising.

The rise of supermarkets, accompanied by expansive parking lots, has not been confined to urban spaces but has extended its reach into suburbs and even far-flung rural areas. This trend has generated considerable wealth for entrepreneurs and property owners astute enough to capitalize on it. In particular, property owners who discerned the potential value addition accompanying the supermarket trend found themselves riding the wave of success.

Consider the compelling story of a lone woman residing on a meager twenty-acre plot largely dominated by scrub pine. When she contemplated selling her modest homestead, discouraging advice and underwhelming offers from local real estate agents clouded her prospects. However, this resilient woman refused to succumb to pessimism. Instead, she embarked on a dedicated thirty-day exploration of the possibilities hidden within rundown farms.

Within this short period, her astute investigation unearthed lucrative prospects for her property. Recognizing the potential for a riding stable complete with pastures and scenic trails, she secured a sale at twice the offer initially proposed by the real estate agent. Impressively, her visionary foresight didn't end there. Through meticulous examination of local supermarkets, she perceived an opportunity for her land to serve as an ideal site for such a commercial venture. Consequently, she sold her farm to a supermarket chain for a staggering five times the original offer.

The endurance of mail-order businesses like Sears, Roebuck, and Montgomery Ward in the face of modern advancements, such as paved roads and accessible automobile transportation, is quite remarkable. Despite the ease of purchasing items directly from stores, these mail-order firms persist and thrive, offering an extensive array of goods, from household items to food, vitamins, hobby supplies, and much more, all delivered right to the consumer's doorstep.

The continued success of mail-order businesses can be attributed to a fundamental truth: while times change, basic human needs persist. The convenience of simply jotting down one's name and address on an order form, dropping it in the mail, and receiving desired goods promptly remains an appealing and efficient way to connect producers with consumers.

In this realm of commerce, direct sales from producers to consumers do occur, yet the prevailing model often involves consumers purchasing from retail middlemen or manufacturer representatives. These intermediaries play a crucial role in facilitating transactions, offering specialized services in retail sales or acting as liaisons between manufacturers and consumers.

Reflecting on this, consider your own potential strategies to bridge the gap between producers and consumers. How might you leverage various channels or methods to facilitate direct connections or optimize the intermediary role in these transactions? Think about innovative approaches that cater to the changing needs and preferences of both producers and consumers in today's dynamic market landscape.

The exploration of wealth accumulation and peace of mind is far from exhaustive. You might even sense that I've merely skimmed the surface of this expansive subject. However, consider revisiting the previous discussions and contemplate how they resonate with your own experiences. Take a broader perspective, stretch the boundaries of interpretation, and you'll discover their remarkable applicability across diverse business scenarios and a wide spectrum of opportunities.

What's fascinating is their universal nature—they aren't tethered to any specific trade or expertise but rather serve as guiding principles adaptable to numerous fields. Engage in a thoughtful exercise of introspection. Explore how these principles align with your personal encounters in business or consumer roles. When you put aside your occupational lens and view yourself solely as a consumer, you'll likely find ample resonance with these principles.

This is merely a prelude to a broader discussion. In the subsequent discussions, we'll delve into additional fundamental principles that successful individuals employ to amass wealth through diligent efforts. Despite the shift in focus, the underlying theme remains constant: the intricate interplay between money and the attainment of inner peace. Stay tuned as we unravel more insights that intertwine the pursuit of financial success with the quest for tranquility and contentment.

Burden of excessive debt can unquestionably disrupt one's tranquility. Initially, you might manage to maintain a semblance of peace, yet debt has a way of insidiously infiltrating your thoughts, occasionally unsettling your mental equilibrium. It's akin to feeling a fraction less in control, sensing that a portion of your autonomy is no longer entirely your own but rather held by someone else. I'm specifically addressing personal debts here, distinct from the typical credit involved in business operations, which is often essential for its functioning.

Building a financial cushion through savings serves as a shield against the unpredictability and potential discomfort accompanying personal indebtedness. However, the value of saving transcends the mere accumulation of funds for future use. It cultivates a valuable habit—the habit of assessing your finances in relation to your necessities. Saving acts as a constant reminder that the essence of money lies not in its possession but in its ability to procure goods and services essential for a fulfilling life.

By engaging in the act of saving, you instinctively discern the true worth of money, understanding its ultimate purpose in facilitating a comfortable existence. Moreover, it prompts introspection into your genuine requirements concerning goods and services, guiding you in distinguishing between what you truly need and what may be merely desirable.

8

THE MASTER MIND

Napoleon Hill

Understanding success often requires adeptly navigating life's dynamic and diverse landscapes with a sense of equilibrium and poise. This journey toward success hinges on harmonizing oneself with the constantly shifting environments. This course acts as a guiding blueprint leading individuals straight to triumph by enabling them to decipher, comprehend, and harness the influential forces shaping their lives.

Even the most triumphant individuals on this planet had to confront and rectify certain shortcomings within their personalities before their ascent to success. These impediments, such as intolerance, cupidity, greed, jealousy, suspicion, revenge, egotism, conceit, the tendency to benefit without effort, and the habit of overspending, often stand as barriers between individuals and their achievements. The Law of Success course meticulously addresses these common adversaries, offering an easily accessible path for individuals of reasonable intellect to conquer them with minimal effort or disruption.

It's essential to note that the Law of Success course transcends the experimental phase; its track record of accomplishments deserves serious consideration and scrutiny. Furthermore, this course has garnered scrutiny and commendation from some of the most pragmatic minds of our time, solidifying its credibility and efficacy.

Originally conceived as a lecture series, the Law of Success course traversed numerous cities and even smaller locales across the United States for over seven years. It's possible that you might have been among the hundreds of thousands who attended these enlightening lectures, witnessing firsthand the transformative potential this course carries.

Throughout these lectures, the author strategically stationed assistants within the audiences to keenly gauge and interpret the immediate reactions of those in attendance. This insightful approach allowed the author to intricately understand the precise impact of the lectures on the audience, leading to subsequent adjustments and enhancements based on meticulous study and analysis.

A significant milestone for the Law of Success philosophy emerged when the author employed it as the foundational material for a course that trained a cohort of 3,000 individuals as a formidable sales force. What's remarkable is that the majority of these participants had no prior experience whatsoever in the realm of sales. Yet, through this comprehensive training program, they achieved a collective earning surpassing One Million Dollars ($1,000,000.00) for themselves. Additionally, they compensated the author a sum of $30,000.00 for his services rendered over an approximate six-month period.

The successes achieved by countless individuals and smaller groups of salespeople who utilized this course as a catalyst for their accomplishments are too extensive to list exhaustively within this Introduction. Nonetheless, the sheer number and the tangible benefits they derived from the course were notably impactful and transformative.

Moreover, the Law of Success philosophy captured the attention of the late Don R. Mellett, the former publisher of the Canton (Ohio) Daily News. Mellett was so captivated by this philosophy that he intended to forge a partnership with the author, preparing to resign from his position as publisher of the Canton Daily News to focus on managing the author's affairs. Tragically, this intention was cut short when Mellett was assassinated on July 16, 1926, leaving a profound impact on the author's endeavors.

In the period before his passing, Mr. Mellett had made arrangements with Judge Elbert H. Gary, who held the esteemed position of Chairman of the Board at the United States Steel Corporation, to introduce the Law of Success course to every employee within the corporation. The planned investment for this initiative amounted to approximately $150,000. Unfortunately, the untimely demise of Judge Gary brought a halt to this significant plan. Nevertheless, this endeavor stands as a testament to the enduring educational value offered by the author of the Law of Success. Judge Gary's thorough analysis of the Law of Success philosophy and his preparedness to commit such a substantial sum as $150,000.00 to it validates the credibility and efficacy of this course.

Within this section of the course, you might encounter a few technical terms that could initially appear unfamiliar or complex. Don't be deterred by this; there's no need to grasp these terms upon your initial reading. As you progress through the rest of the course, these terms will naturally become clearer and more understandable. This Introduction primarily serves as a backdrop for the subsequent fifteen lessons, and it's intended for you to read it as such. There's no examination focused on this Introduction, but revisiting it multiple times will likely reveal new thoughts or ideas with each reading that you may have overlooked previously.

This Introduction illuminates a newly unearthed psychological law that forms the cornerstone of remarkable personal achievements. The author refers to this law as the "Master Mind," signifying a developed mindset arising from the harmonious collaboration of two or more individuals united with the aim of accomplishing a specific task.

For those involved in the sales profession, the "Master Mind" law presents an intriguing opportunity for experimentation in their daily endeavors. Remarkable outcomes have been observed when a group of six or seven salespeople effectively harness this law, leading to remarkable boosts in their sales performance that might appear unbelievable at first glance.

Life insurance, despite being an established necessity, paradoxically ranks as one of the most challenging products to sell. This quirk of the market persists, even though the need for life insurance is undeniable. However, a small collective of agents from the Prudential Life Insurance Company, specializing in smaller policies, decided to pool their efforts and experiment with the law of the "Master Mind." Astonishingly, within the initial three months of this trial, every member of this group achieved sales volumes surpassing their entire year's worth of performance before the experiment.

The potential unleashed by applying this principle within a small, intelligent group of life insurance salespeople is awe-inspiring. The profound impact of this principle, when effectively employed, has the capacity to exceed the most optimistic expectations and imagination.

Similarly, this concept isn't limited to life insurance; it extends to other groups of sales professionals dealing in tangible products and services. Consider this as you delve into the Introduction to the Law of Success course. There's a reasonable chance that just this Introduction could impart enough insight into the law of the "Master Mind" to substantially redirect the trajectory of your life.

THE ART OF SELLING YOURSELF

The success of a business often hinges on the personalities behind it. The way these personalities are tailored to be more appealing and engaging to patrons can significantly impact the thriving nature of the business. In bustling American cities, numerous stores offer similar goods at comparable prices, yet one store consistently outperforms others. This success is attributed to the individuals steering the store, who have dedicated themselves to refining the personalities that interact with the public. It's noteworthy that consumers are just as inclined to buy into these personalities as they are to purchase merchandise. In fact, the influence of these personalities might surpass that of the actual products.

Interestingly, the life insurance industry has evolved to a level of scientific precision where the cost of insurance remains relatively consistent, regardless of the provider. Despite this uniformity, only a select few companies, fewer than a dozen, dominate the life insurance market in the United States, controlling the majority of the business. This goes to show that even within a realm of standardized products, the personalities, approaches, and strategies of these companies play a pivotal role in consumer preferences and choices.

Consider this: nearly ninety-nine out of every hundred life insurance policy buyers aren't fully acquainted with the contents of their policies. More surprising, they don't seem particularly bothered by this fact. What they're truly investing in is the captivating and relatable personality of an agent who comprehends the significant value of nurturing such an appealing persona.

Now, let's talk about success—the pinnacle of your life's pursuits and, per the essence defined in this course on the Fifteen Laws of Success, achieving your Definite Chief Aim without infringing upon others' rights. Whatever your primary objective in life might be, attaining it becomes notably easier once you've mastered the art of cultivating a pleasing personality. This art isn't just about individual charm but also revolves around establishing effective alliances without encountering friction or jealousy, a skill vital for successful collaborations.

Arguably, one of life's most pressing challenges is mastering the art of negotiating with others harmoniously. This course stands as a beacon, guiding individuals toward navigating life with grace and balance, steering clear of the damaging repercussions of conflicts and disputes that annually lead millions to despair, scarcity, and failure.

As you delve into these lessons, consider them as the catalyst for an imminent and comprehensive transformation in your personality, paving the way for a more harmonious and successful journey ahead.

The premise of enjoying extraordinary success in life invariably links to wielding power, a facet that's inseparable from possessing a commanding personality that entices others to collaborate harmoniously with you.

The evolution termed "civilization" stands as a gauge reflecting the cumulative knowledge amassed by humankind. This knowledge, broadly categorized into two classes, encompasses both mental and physical dimensions.

In the realm of organized knowledge, humanity has systematically unveiled and documented over eighty physical elements that constitute the fundamental building blocks of all material forms throughout the cosmos. This classification and understanding of the physical elements serve as a testament to humanity's relentless pursuit and comprehension of the underlying structures of existence.

MIND'S BUILDING BLOCKS

Exploring the vast expanse of the material universe, humans have delved into its enormity, uncovering planets, suns, and stars that tower over our humble Earth, some eclipsing it by ten millionfold in size.

Conversely, the quest for understanding has also unveiled the minuteness inherent within the physical forms constituting this universe. Boiling down the eighty-odd physical elements, scientists have dissected them into molecules, atoms, and eventually to the minutest entity—the electron. While invisible to the naked eye, an electron embodies a core of energy, existing either in a positive or negative charge, serving as the genesis of all physical entities.

Engaging with the fundamentals of knowledge acquisition, it becomes imperative for students to commence their journey with these foundational particles of physical matter. These particles serve as the rudimentary building blocks wielded by Nature in crafting the entire framework of the physical cosmos.

Molecules, Atoms and Electrons

At the molecular level, atoms are the crux, perceived as inconspicuous fragments of matter ceaselessly orbiting at lightning speed, echoing the orbital dance akin to Earth's rotation around the sun.

These minute constituents, atoms, coursing perpetually

within a molecule, are purportedly composed of electrons—these being the elemental specks of physical matter. As earlier mentioned, an electron signifies a duality of force, uniform in class, size, and nature, duplicating the fundamental principles that underpin the entire cosmos within the confines of a grain of sand or a drop of water.

The profundity and vastness of this scientific reality are truly astonishing! Imagine, as you sit down to enjoy a meal, each morsel you savor, the very plate and utensils that hold your food, and even the table upon which it rests—all distill down to a meticulous assembly of electrons.

From the grandest celestial bodies adrift in the heavens to the most minuscule speck of sand adorning the Earth's surface, the entire spectrum of physical matter is an intricate ballet of molecules, atoms, and electrons ceaselessly gyrating at unimaginable speeds.

Unveiling the perpetual vibrancy of physical matter, it's essential to note that nothing remains stagnant; even though to the naked eye, the majority of physical matter may seem motionless. Indeed, no entity embodies absolute solidity. Consider the hardest steel; it's merely an amalgamation of dynamic molecules, atoms, and electrons engaged in perpetual motion. Fascinatingly, electrons within steel, gold, silver, brass, or pewter share the same inherent nature and whirl at identical speeds, showcasing the consistency of this universal building block, albeit their varied arrangements in different materials. The intriguing aspect lies in the distinct compositions of these materials, formed by unique combinations of atoms while preserving the uniformity of electrons, albeit some being positively charged and others negatively charged, representing a dichotomy in electrification.

The realm of chemistry unveils the immutable nature of

atoms, the fundamental constituents of matter, which remain unalterable within themselves. This scientific study delineates the creation of the myriad of eighty-odd elements through the manipulation and arrangement of these unchanging atoms. Picture the intricate dance of chemistry, where subtle adjustments in atomic positions give birth to new elements: introducing four electrons—two positive and two negative—into a hydrogen atom miraculously transforms it into lithium. On the contrary, extracting a positive and a negative electron from the lithium atom converts it into a helium atom, marking the shift from one element to another.

This symphony of change illustrates that the varied physical elements of the universe distinguish themselves solely by the electron count in their atoms and the configuration of these atoms within each element's molecules. Imagine the atomic composition of mercury housing eighty positive and eighty negative electrons. Should a chemist remove two positive electrons, the very essence would transform into platinum. Furthermore, by expelling an additional negative electron, the mercury atom would lose two positive charges, maintaining seventy-nine positive charges within the nucleus and seventy-nine negative electrons, metamorphosing into the illustrious metal—gold!

For aeons, alchemists and modern chemists alike have fervently pursued the elusive formula to orchestrate such electronic transformations. A profound fact acknowledged by chemists is that from merely four types of atoms—hydrogen, oxygen, nitrogen, and carbon—sprout forth myriads of synthetic substances, amounting to tens of thousands, encapsulating the astonishing diversity of matter itself.

Intricacies within atoms, specifically variations in electron counts, underlie the distinctive chemical traits that atoms of the same element possess. Despite their similarities within an element, differences in electron numbers and their arrangement within molecules give rise to both physical and chemical disparities among compounds. Substances, seemingly disparate, can be formed from the same kinds of atoms but in varying compositions, resulting in a plethora of compounds.

The minute nuances within molecules have colossal implications; the removal of a single atom from certain substances can transmute them from life-sustaining compounds into lethal poisons. Consider phosphorus—an element comprising identical atoms, yet exhibiting color variations, like yellow or red, contingent upon the spatial configuration of its molecules.

It's an absolute reality that the atom stands as nature's universal building block, the elemental particle with which all material structures, from the tiniest grain of sand to the mightiest star in the cosmos, are fashioned. In its infinitesimal form, the atom serves as the foundational unit from which nature assembles the grandeur of an oak tree or a pine, the robustness of sandstone or granite, and the diversity of life, be it a mouse or an elephant.

The fascinating hypotheses of some profound thinkers propose that the genesis of our planet and every elemental entity dwelling upon it originated from the union of two atoms. Over hundreds of millions of years hurtling through the celestial expanse, these atoms, they surmise, incessantly attracted and amassed other atoms, progressively fashioning the very foundation of our planet. This hypothesis purports to explain the diverse layers composing Earth's crust, from coal beds and iron ore deposits to the treasury of gold, silver, and copper reserves.

Their theory suggests that as Earth traversed space, it intercepted a spectrum of nebulous entities or atoms, swiftly appropriating them due to the laws of magnetic attraction. While the theory lacks irrefutable evidence, the Earth's composition does offer intriguing clues that lend credence to this supposition.

These foundational principles regarding the minuscule constituents of matter serve as the point of departure from which we embark upon an exploration of harnessing and deploying the principles of POWER.

Observations underscore the perpetual state of motion or vibration that pervades all matter. Molecules consist of rapidly oscillating entities known as atoms, which in turn are comprised of swiftly moving particles termed electrons.

The Vibrating Fluid of Matter

The ethereal essence permeating each fragment of matter manifests as an imperceptible yet dynamic "fluid" or force that precipitates atoms into a ceaseless orbit around one another at an unfathomable velocity.

This enigmatic "fluid" remains an enigma, confounding the scientific community and eluding comprehensive analysis. Some scholars align its essence with the properties of electricity, while others lean towards defining it as vibration. A prevailing hypothesis contends that the velocity at which this force, or "fluid energy," moves significantly dictates the observable characteristics of physical entities in the universe.

Remarkably, varying rates of vibration of this dynamic "fluid energy" yield different manifestations. At lower frequencies, it translates into sound, perceptible to the human ear within the range of 32,000 to 38,000 vibrations per second. As this frequency ascends beyond the audible spectrum, the energy metamorphoses into heat, typically commencing at approximately 1,500,000 vibrations per second.

When ascending the vibration scale, the progression unfolds, transcending into the domain of light as it reaches around 3,000,000 vibrations per second, generating the radiant hues of violet. Beyond this threshold, vibrations venture into the realm of the unseen, projecting ultra-violet rays and other imperceptible radiations, veiled to the naked eye.

Venturing even higher on this expansive scale—where the precise pinnacle remains elusive—vibrations seem to birth the very essence of human thought. The author contends that this fundamental "fluid" component underpinning all vibrations, the genesis of all known energy forms, is universal in its essence. It is proposed that the "fluid" element propelling sound mirrors that of light, with their distinction lying solely in the pace of their vibrational frequencies. Furthermore, the "fluid" essence driving thought is purportedly akin to that found in sound, heat, and light, diverging primarily in their frequency of vibrations per second. Just as there exists one fundamental form of physical matter— the electron—that constitutes the substance of Earth, planets, stars, and celestial bodies, the concept extends to this singular essence of "fluid" energy, propelling all matter into perpetual motion.

Air and Ether

In the vast expanse of interstellar space, between celestial bodies like suns, moons, stars, and planets, lies a pervasive energy known as ether. The author posits a belief that the intrinsic "fluid" energy driving the perpetual motion of all matter aligns with this universal "fluid" termed ether, which permeates every corner of the cosmos. A defined layer encircling the Earth, estimated at around fifty miles, constitutes the breathable substance called air, a gaseous blend of oxygen and nitrogen. While air aptly transmits sound vibrations, it serves as a barrier against light and the higher vibrations that traverse the realms of ether. Ether, conversely, acts as a conduit for all vibrations from sound to the realms of thought.

Air, localized within a specific radius, primarily caters to sustaining both plant and animal life by supplying essential oxygen and nitrogen, crucial for their existence. Nitrogen remains pivotal for plant growth, whereas oxygen stands as a cornerstone for animal survival. At extreme altitudes, such as mountaintops, air becomes significantly lighter due to a reduction in nitrogen content, rendering plant life unsustainable in such conditions. In contrast, the "light" air prevalent at higher elevations comprises a greater proportion of oxygen, a reason why high altitudes are recommended for patients with conditions like tuberculosis.

Though this foundational understanding may lack the dramatic flair of a captivating fiction, your commitment lies in uncovering your inherent capabilities and mastering their organization and application. Success in this endeavor hinges on a blend of determination, unwavering persistence, and a resolute desire to gather and structure knowledge effectively.

EVERY MIND BOTH A BROADCASTING AND A RECEIVING STATION

This author, through countless instances, has found convincing evidence, at least to his own satisfaction, that every human brain operates as both a transmitter and a receiver for thought vibrations.

Should this theory be substantiated as factual and methods of reasonable control established, envision the profound impact it could wield in the acquisition, classification, and organization of knowledge. The mere potential, let alone the likelihood, of such a reality, boggles the human mind!

Thomas Paine, a luminary of the American Revolutionary Period, holds immense credit for initiating and concluding the Revolution. His sharp intellect not only contributed to the drafting of the Declaration of Independence but also persuaded its signatories to transform it from mere words on parchment into tangible reality.

Thomas Paine, when discussing the origin of his vast reservoir of knowledge, articulated it in this manner:

Any individual observing the progression of the human mind, through their own experiences, must discern two distinct classes of thoughts: those engendered by introspection and conscious contemplation, and those that spontaneously infiltrate the mind. I have adhered to the principle of treating these unbidden thoughts with courtesy, diligently scrutinizing if they were worth harboring; it is from them that I have gleaned nearly all my knowledge. The education received from traditional schooling merely serves as a starting point, a modest foundation allowing one to embark on self-initiated learning thereafter. Ultimately, every erudite person becomes their own mentor, as principles cannot be merely imprinted onto memory; they find their abode in comprehension, and their permanence originates from conception.

In those insightful words, Thomas Paine, the eminent American patriot and philosopher, articulated an occurrence that resonates with virtually every individual at some point in their lives. It's a common experience to receive irrefutable evidence that thoughts or even entire concepts unexpectedly manifest within one's mind from external sources.

How do these thoughts arrive? What conduit could possibly exist for such visitors if not the ether? This boundless substance permeates the vast expanse of the universe, acting as the conduit for various known forms of vibration—sound, light, and heat. Might it also serve as the pathway for the transmission of Thought?

Each mind, each brain, finds direct connection to every other brain through this ethereal medium. Any thought unleashed by one brain can instantaneously be intercepted and comprehended by all other brains in harmonious resonance with the originating brain. The certainty of this principle is as solid for this author as the knowledge that the chemical formula (H_2O) produces water. Contemplate the profound role this principle plays across every facet of existence.

The potential role of the ether as a conduit for the transmission of thoughts from one mind to another is just one of its potentially astounding functionalities. According to this author's belief, every thought vibration originating from any brain is intercepted by the ether, perpetually circulating in intricate waveforms whose lengths correspond to the energy utilized during their emission. These vibrations, perpetually in motion, exist as one of the dual sources from which thoughts spontaneously emerge within one's mind. The other source being direct, immediate contact facilitated by the ether with the brain that initiated the thought vibration.

Consider the implication: if this theory holds true, the vast expanse of the universe becomes, and will forever be, an expansive mental repository. Within this ethereal library resides an accumulation of thoughts released by humanity. This concept forms the cornerstone of one of the pivotal hypotheses outlined in the lesson on Self-confidence—a crucial point for the student to bear in mind when delving into that particular lesson.

Nature's Bible, an eternal testament encapsulating the history of the human race and the birth of civilization, remains a source of profound wisdom and knowledge. The narrative of our civilization's evolution is inscribed within the elemental constituents of our planet and the ether that pervades the cosmos.

In the pursuit of understanding, humanity has delved into the sedimentary layers of this earth, unearthing relics—bones, footprints, and fossils—an unequivocal testament to the history of life on this planet. These enigmatic remnants serve as a beacon, meticulously placed by Mother Nature, guiding and enlightening us through unfathomable epochs.

This expansive and timeless manuscript, manifested in the stone-carved pages of our planet and the intangible pages of the ether, embodies an authentic channel of communication between the divine Creator and humankind. Commencing its narrative long before the inception of human thought, even preceding the emergence of the amoeba, Nature's Bible holds the ancient wisdom that echoes throughout the ages.

The integrity of Nature's Bible, impervious to any human intervention or manipulation, allows its timeless wisdom to be conveyed through a universal language accessible to all who can perceive it. This unchanging repository of knowledge remains unblemished and unaltered throughout time, offering an invaluable source of wisdom and insight.

The recent unveiling of the radio principle, operating within the ethereal realm, serves as a remarkable testament to the profound mysteries encapsulated within Nature's Bible. The ethereal medium, capable of seamlessly converting commonplace sound vibrations into radio frequencies, traverses vast expanses of space, carrying these transmissions across great distances, and restores them to their original audible form within an infinitesimal period. This astonishing capability hints at the potential for thought vibrations to be similarly retained and transmitted indefinitely, a notion that aligns with the ether's extraordinary prowess.

The established reality of instantaneous sound transmission through the ether using modern radio technologies provides tangible evidence supporting the notion of thoughts transcending minds. This elevation of the concept from a mere possibility to a probable phenomenon lends credence to the idea that our thoughts may indeed traverse the boundless expanse of the ether, fostering an interconnectedness beyond conventional understanding.

THE MASTER MIND

When delving into the methodology of gathering, categorizing, and structuring valuable knowledge, a significant progression emerges through the harmonious integration of multiple minds, culminating in the formation of a Master Mind.

The concept of the "Master Mind" is a somewhat abstract notion, lacking a direct counterpart within the known realms of established facts. Its recognition and understanding are confined to a select few individuals who have devoted themselves to meticulously examining the influence exerted by one mind upon others.

Despite exhaustive searches through various textbooks and scholarly essays centered on the human mind, no mention or allusion to the concept of the "Master Mind" has been unearthed by this author. The term was initially brought to the author's attention during an encounter with Andrew Carnegie, as outlined in Lesson Two. This encounter served as the impetus for exploring and comprehending the profound implications of this extraordinary principle.

CHEMISTRY OF THE MIND

The author holds a belief in the mind's composition as being akin to the universal "fluid" energy prevalent in the ether permeating the cosmos. An intriguing fact, widely acknowledged among both the general populace and scientific circles, is the immediate clash or profound resonance experienced when certain minds intersect, showcasing a spectrum of reactions.

In the realm of mind interactions, a broad spectrum exists between the extreme poles of natural affinity and inherent antagonism. Some minds effortlessly gravitate toward one another, resulting in an instantaneous and profound connection—often referred to as "love at first sight." Conversely, there are instances where minds repel vehemently upon initial contact, leading to mutual antipathy. These reactions manifest without verbal exchanges or recognizable cues typically associated with the catalysts of affection or animosity.

Consideration of the mind's potential composition—whether a fluid, substance, or energy analogous to or perhaps synonymous with the ether—provides fertile ground for exploration. When two minds converge and establish a connection, it's conceivable that the amalgamation of these "mind substances" (akin to ether's electrons) triggers a chemical reaction, initiating vibrations that elicit either pleasurable or discordant effects on the individuals involved.

The impact of the convergence of two minds is evident even to the most casual observer. In search of causality for such changes in mental attitudes following a close interaction, one might reasonably speculate that this shift results from the disturbance and reorganization of electrons or mental units within each mind when exposed to the new field formed by their contact.

Establishing a lesson upon a solid foundation involves acknowledging that when two minds meet or closely engage, a noticeable shift occurs in each mind's state, distinct from their state immediately before contact. While understanding the precise "cause" of this mind-to-mind reaction might be desirable, it's not essential. However, the undeniable fact remains that such reactions occur, offering a starting point to elucidate the concept of a "Master Mind."

The concept of a Master Mind emerges through the deliberate blending of two or more minds in a seamless spirit of harmony. This harmonious amalgamation creates a third mind through a mental chemistry, one that can be embraced and utilized by any or all of the individual minds involved. This Master Mind persists as long as the amicable and harmonious alliance between the individual minds endures. However, once this alliance fractures, the Master Mind disintegrates, and all traces of its former existence vanish instantaneously.

In exploring the principle of mind chemistry, it's evident that this very principle underlies many often-debated cases of "soul-mates" and "eternal triangles," situations that unfortunately land in divorce courts, only to be met with mockery and scandalous chatter from those ignorant of Nature's profound laws.

The universally acknowledged truth that the initial years of marriage frequently entail petty disagreements is well-known across civilized societies. These are regarded as the crucial years of "adjustment." Surviving this phase often cements a marriage into a lasting alliance. Experienced married individuals readily attest to these facts, though the deeper causes behind this phenomenon remain less understood.

Among the contributing factors to the lack of harmony during these early marriage years, the gradual blending of minds' chemistry stands as a predominant cause. Initially, the electrons or mental units may not exhibit extreme friendliness or antagonism upon first interaction. With continued association, they slowly adapt to harmonize, except in rare instances where prolonged interaction leads to outright hostility between these mental units.

Remarkably, after a decade or more of living together, couples often become indispensable to each other, even in the absence of overt expressions of love. Interestingly, this long-term association, including the intimate relationship, not only fosters a natural affinity between the minds but also induces striking similarities in facial expressions and other discernible traits. A skilled observer of human nature can easily discern the spouse in a crowd of strangers, having been introduced to their partner, owing to the shared expressions, facial contours, and even the tonality of their voices.

The fascinating dynamics of the human mind's chemistry hold a profound impact, so much so that a seasoned public speaker can swiftly discern the reception of their statements by an audience. Even the slightest trace of antagonism among a thousand listeners becomes palpable to the speaker who's learned to sense and interpret these reactions. Remarkably, this insight doesn't rely on observing facial expressions; an audience can either elevate a speaker to sublime oratorical heights or dishearten them into failure, all without displaying a single sign of contentment or discontentment on their faces.

The realm of "Master Salesmen" holds a similar mastery; they discern the precise psychological moment for closing a deal not from the words of the potential buyer, but from the subtle cues and reactions felt within the chemistry of their mind. Unlike words that can mask intentions, interpreting mental chemistry leaves no room for ambiguity. It's a common understanding among adept salespeople that most buyers tend to adopt a negative stance almost until the pinnacle of a sale.

Likewise, proficient lawyers have honed a sort of sixth sense that enables them to navigate through meticulously chosen words of a clever yet dishonest witness. Their ability to accurately interpret the true thoughts of a witness, based on mental chemistry, showcases a profound understanding, almost an intuition. Interestingly, many lawyers and salespeople have developed this remarkable skill without necessarily comprehending its scientific foundation; they possess the technique without a comprehensive scientific understanding of its basis.

An individual adept in understanding the intricacies of mental chemistry possesses a remarkable ability akin to strolling into the grand mansion of another person's mind and leisurely exploring its corridors and rooms. They can meticulously observe its minutiae, departing with a comprehensive understanding of the entire interior without the mind's owner realizing they've been visited. This principle, highlighted in the lesson on Accurate Thinking, showcases the practical utilization of comprehending mental chemistry as an approach to the core principles of this lesson.

Sufficient groundwork has been laid to introduce the concept of mind chemistry, underscoring how when two minds closely interact, a perceptible mental shift occurs—sometimes manifesting as antagonism, while at other times as friendliness. Every mind generates an "electric field," the nature of which hinges upon the mind's underlying mood and the chemistry creating this field.

The author posits that an individual's mental chemistry is a blend of their physical heredity and the dominant thoughts that have influenced their mind over time. Moreover, every mind remains in a state of continuous flux as one's philosophical outlook and habitual thoughts consistently reshape the mind's chemistry. While these principles are held as beliefs by the author, it's a known fact that an individual can consciously alter their mind's chemistry to either attract or repel those they encounter. Remarkably, an individual can assume a mental disposition capable of drawing others towards them in a pleasing manner or causing aversion and antagonism—without reliance on words, facial expressions, or any form of physical comportment.

Delve back into the essence of a "Master Mind"—a culmination of two or more minds coming together in a spirit of absolute harmony, and you'll grasp the profound significance of "harmony" as applied here. Without this perfect alignment, two minds fail to blend or coordinate effectively. It underscores the pivotal role of harmony in determining the success or failure of business and social partnerships.

Across various domains—be it sales management, military command, or leadership in any other sphere—the imperative of an "esprit de corps," a collective spirit of understanding and collaboration, is universally recognized in achieving success. This unified spirit emerges from a form of discipline, be it voluntary or coerced, that brings individual minds together into what's referred to as a "Master Mind." In this context, individual mental chemistry undergoes modification, enabling these minds to merge and operate as a single entity.

The methods employed to facilitate this blending process vary widely among leaders, each crafting their unique approach to coordinating the minds of their followers. Some resort to force, while others rely on persuasion. Some leverage the fear of penalties, while others emphasize rewards, all aiming to amalgamate individual minds into a cohesive whole. Exploring historical accounts in statesmanship, politics, business, or finance unveils the diverse techniques employed by leaders in amalgamating individual minds into a collective consciousness.

Principle Behind Mind Chemistry

Let's delve into the realm of exceptional leadership. Among the great leaders throughout history, there are those bestowed by Nature with an innate combination of mind chemistry that serves as a magnetic nucleus attracting other minds. Napoleon stands as a prime illustration, possessing a magnetic mind type that inherently drew all minds within its reach. The impelling nature of his personality, nothing more than the chemistry of his mind, led soldiers to follow him even into perilous situations without hesitation.

However, it's crucial to recognize that no collective of minds can form a Master Mind if one individual among them exhibits an extremely negative or repellent mindset. The dynamics of a Master Mind hinge on the cohesive blending of minds, and when there's a stark contrast between negative and positive mentalities, true harmony and synthesis cannot occur. Regrettably, the unawareness of this reality has led many otherwise capable leaders to face defeat despite their competence.

Able leaders well-versed in the dynamics of mind chemistry possess the ability to temporarily amalgamate the minds of diverse groups, forming what appears to be a cohesive mass mind. However, this amalgamation tends to disintegrate almost instantly once the leader steps away from the group's sphere. Consider some of the most prosperous life insurance sales organizations and other sales forces; they convene regularly, often weekly or even more frequently, for a specific purpose—But what exactly is that purpose?

FOR THE PURPOSE OF MERGING THE INDIVIDUAL MINDS INTO A MASTER MIND WHICH WILL, FOR A

LIMITED NUMBER OF DAYS, SERVE AS A STIMULUS TO THE INDIVIDUAL MINDS!

In these instances, it's often the case that the leaders orchestrating these gatherings, typically referred to as "pep meetings," may not fully grasp the intricate dynamics occurring within. Such meetings generally follow a pattern where leaders and members engage in talks, occasionally hosting external speakers. However, the core essence of these meetings lies beyond the surface.

The human brain operates akin to an electric battery, susceptible to exhaustion or depletion, leading individuals to feel despondent and lacking in vigor—emotions most of us have experienced. When the brain reaches this state, it requires a recharge, and this replenishment is attained through contact with more vibrant and energetic minds. Proficient leaders comprehend the crucial nature of this "recharging" process and possess the skill to effectuate it. This understanding stands as the quintessential trait distinguishing a leader from a mere follower.

Understanding this principle becomes a boon for individuals who comprehend the significance of keeping their brains vitalized or "recharged" by periodically engaging with more dynamic minds. Sexual contact, when intelligently undertaken between individuals sharing genuine affection, stands as one of the most effective stimuli for revitalization. However, it's crucial to note that any other form of sexual relationship can deplete the mind instead of invigorating it. Remarkably, adept practitioners in Psycho-therapeutics have the ability to reinvigorate a brain within a short span.

Touching upon the aspect of sexual contact as a means of revitalization, it's noteworthy that virtually all great leaders throughout history, irrespective of their domain, have possessed highly active and vibrant sexual natures. The term "sex" might raise eyebrows but is not inherently indecent; indeed, it's a term commonly found in dictionaries.

A shift is discernible among well-informed physicians and health practitioners who are increasingly inclined to accept the theory that diseases manifest when an individual's brain is in a depleted or devitalized state. Put differently, a perfectly vitalized brain renders an individual practically immune, if not entirely, from various diseases.

Understanding that "Nature" or the mind plays a pivotal role in curing diseases is a fundamental concept embraced by intelligent health practitioners across diverse fields. While medicines, faith, alternative therapies like chiropractic or osteopathy, and other external interventions exist, they primarily serve as catalysts or aids to Nature's inherent curative powers. They simply ignite the chemistry of the mind, facilitating the realignment of cells and tissues in the body, revitalizing the brain, and restoring normal functionality to the human machine.

Even the most traditional medical practitioner acknowledges the truth in this understanding.

This realization prompts us to ponder the future prospects within the realm of mind chemistry. Envisioning a world where the harmonious blending of minds fosters optimal health becomes a plausible vision. Moreover, harnessing this principle holds the potential to generate adequate power to alleviate the constant economic strains that individuals face. The amalgamation of minds in harmony might hold the key to overcoming the persistent pressures of economic stressors.

We may judge the future possibilities of mind chemistry by taking inventory of its past achievements, keeping in mind the fact that these achievements have been largely the result of accidental discovery and of chance groupings of minds. We are approaching the time when the professorate of the universities will teach mind chemistry the same as other subjects are now taught. Meanwhile, study and experimentation in connection with this subject open vistas of possibility for the individual student.

9

THE REALIZATION OF PROSPERITY

James Allen

Indeed, genuine prosperity finds its roots within a heart enriched with integrity, trust, generosity, and love. It's a truth that prosperity, much like happiness, doesn't solely reside in material possessions but rather thrives as an inner realization.

Consider the plight of the greedy individual who may amass wealth but remains eternally wretched, living in a state of inner poverty despite external affluence. His wealth cannot bring contentment, for as long as someone else possesses more, he sees himself as impoverished. On the other hand, those embodying honesty, generosity, and love find themselves immersed in a wealth that transcends material possessions. Their inner richness and contentment flourish, even if their external possessions are modest.

The definition of true richness transcends mere material possessions. A person's wealth isn't measured by the accumulation of riches but by their contentment with what they possess and their generosity in sharing it.

When we pause to ponder the universe, brimming with abundant treasures—both material and spiritual—and contrast it with humanity's narrow focus on amassing gold or land, it becomes evident how dark and misguided selfishness truly is. Selfish desires ultimately lead to self-destruction, whereas Nature, in its generosity, loses nothing by giving all.

True prosperity isn't found in settling into the belief that doing right leads to everything going wrong. The concept of competition shouldn't shake one's belief in the supremacy of righteousness. While some may tout the laws of competition, I hold steadfast in the unchangeable law that shall one day overturn them. Even now, in the hearts and lives of the righteous, this law undermines the dominance of competition.

1. **Trusting in the Unchangeable Law:** Understanding this Law allows for serene composure even in the face of dishonesty, knowing that it leads to certain destruction. Embrace doing what is believed to be right, trusting in the Divine Power inherent in the universe. This trust ensures constant protection and the conversion of losses into gains, curses into blessings.
2. **The Power of Integrity, Generosity, and Love:** Upholding integrity, generosity, and love, coupled with energy, is the path toward true prosperity. These virtues not only elevate an individual but also transform losses into gains and curses into blessings.
3. **Beyond Self-Centeredness:** Reject the notion that self-centeredness should precede consideration for others. Prioritizing only personal comforts disregards the needs of others. Those who adopt this mentality may find themselves abandoned in their moments of need, isolated without support or aid.
4. **Expanding the Soul and Heart:** Instead, expand your soul and let your heart extend warmth and kindness to others. Such actions will bring enduring joy and usher

in prosperity. By practicing this expansive attitude, one naturally guards against the competitive, self-serving mindset, finding strength and security in pursuing what's right without the need for defensive measures.

5. **Demonstrating Integrity and Faith**: There exist real-life examples of individuals who have triumphed over competition solely through unwavering integrity and faith. Despite facing adversaries and attempts to undermine them, these individuals have maintained their methods and steadily ascended into prosperity. Meanwhile, those attempting to undercut them have ultimately met with defeat.

6. **The Armor of Goodness**: Possessing and nurturing inward qualities synonymous with goodness provides an impregnable armor against the onslaught of evil forces. It acts as a shield, offering double protection during challenging times. Cultivating these qualities not only fortifies personal character but also constructs a success that remains unshakeable, leading to a prosperity that endures indefinitely.

"The White Robe of the Heart Invisible
Is stained with sin and sorrow, grief and pain,
And all repentant pools and springs of prayer
Shall not avail to wash it white again.
While in the path of ignorance I walk,
The stains of error will not cease to cling
Defilements mark the crooked path of self,
Where anguish lurks and disappointments sting.
Knowledge and wisdom only can avail
To purify and make my garment clean,
For therein lie love's waters; therein rests

Peace undisturbed, eternal, and serene.
Sin and repentance is the path of pain,
Knowledge and wisdom is the path of Peace
By the near way of practice I will find
Where bliss begins, how pains and sorrows cease.
Self shall depart, and Truth shall take its place
The Changeless One, the Indivisible
Shall take up His abode in me, and cleanse
The White Robe of the Heart Invisible."

10

THE TWO MASTERS, SELF AND TRUTH

James Allen

The battlefield of the human soul presents an eternal struggle between two dominant forces vying for supremacy and control over the heart's throne: the master of self and the master of Truth. The self, often referred to as the "Prince of this world," represents rebellion and wields weapons of passion, pride, avarice, vanity, and self-will—tools of darkness. On the other side stands Truth, often described as the Father God, embodying meekness and humility. Truth's arsenal consists of gentleness, patience, purity, sacrifice, humility, and love, all instruments of Light.

This conflict unfolds within every soul, much like a soldier who cannot simultaneously engage in two opposing armies. Every heart aligns itself with either the ranks of self or the banner of Truth. There exists no middle ground in this spiritual warfare; the presence of self excludes the presence of Truth, and vice versa. Buddha, the revered teacher of Truth, stated this clearly:

> *There is self and there is Truth; where self is, Truth is not, where Truth is, self is not."* Echoing this sentiment, Jesus, the Christ, proclaimed, *"No man can serve two masters; for*

either he will hate the one and love the other, or else he will hold to the one and despise the other. Ye cannot serve God and Mammon.

The simplicity of Truth stands as an unwavering beacon, devoid of complexities, nuances, or compromises. It remains resolute, unwavering, and unqualified. In stark contrast, self, governed by intricate desires, bends and twists endlessly, allowing for subtle qualifications and turns. Those ensnared by self-deception harbor the false belief that they can pursue worldly desires while simultaneously possessing Truth. However, the devotees of Truth relinquish self, offering it as a sacrifice, and vigilantly guard against the allure of worldliness and self-indulgence.

If your quest is to discover and embody Truth, you must be ready for sacrifices of the utmost degree, to renounce every vestige of self. Truth reveals itself in its entirety only when every trace of self has dissolved.

The eternal teachings of Christ emphasize the necessity for daily self-denial to follow the path of discipleship. Are you prepared to renounce your desires, prejudices, and opinions? If so, the narrow path of Truth opens its gates to you, offering a peace inaccessible to the world. The ultimate state of Truth lies in the complete annihilation of self, a pinnacle reached through various religions and philosophies that serve as aids in attaining this supreme state.

The paradox of self and Truth is vivid: self embodies the negation of Truth, while Truth embodies the denial of self. In the process of self-annihilation, the essence of Truth is resurrected within you. Yet, as you tightly grasp onto self, the brilliance of Truth remains veiled from your sight.

Clutching onto self inevitably leads to a path riddled with obstacles, with recurring afflictions, anguish, and disillusionment as constant companions. Conversely, within the realm of Truth, difficulties cease to exist. Embracing Truth liberates you from the shackles of sorrow and disillusionment.

Truth isn't concealed or obscure in itself. It is perpetually unveiled, perfectly transparent. However, the blinded and misguided self remains unable to apprehend it. Just as daylight remains hidden to the sightless, the Light of Truth remains veiled to those clouded by self.

Truth stands as the singular, immutable reality in the cosmos—an inner symphony, a divine equilibrium, an everlasting love. It stands complete and unalterable. Its existence isn't contingent upon any individual, yet every individual relies upon it. The splendor of Truth remains elusive when viewed through the lens of self. Vanity taints perceptions with its hues, lust distorts views through the lens of desire, and pride and stubborn opinions overshadow the perception of the universe, leaving only the grandeur of one's own views.

A striking disparity distinguishes the seeker of Truth from the one submerged in self: humility. True humility isn't just an absence of vanity, obstinacy, or egotism; it's also recognizing one's opinions as inconsequential. This genuine humility doesn't exalt personal views as ultimate truth but rather acknowledges the vast expanse of what remains unknown.

The individual entrenched in self-righteousness often perceives their opinions as infallible truth, disparaging others' views as fallacious. Conversely, the humble Truth-seeker discerns between mere opinions and the essence of Truth. Such a person views others with compassion, not aiming to defend their opinions but willing to relinquish them for a deeper understanding and embodiment of Truth. For Truth is not a concept to debate; it's a life to be lived. And in this pursuit, charity—boundless love—is the closest one can come to embodying Truth.

Engaging in fervent debates, individuals often assume they champion Truth when, in reality, they defend transient interests and opinions. The self-driven defender enters conflicts against others, while the Truth-seeker confronts the inner conflicts within themselves. Truth, immutable and eternal, remains indifferent to our opinions. We may choose to embrace it or linger outside its domain, yet both our defenses and offenses against it prove futile and recoil upon ourselves.

1. **Religion of Truth versus Worship of Self:** Those captivated by self-righteousness tend to perceive their creed or religion as the only truth, zealously proselytizing others. However, Truth transcends religious formalities; it dwells within an unselfish, sanctified heart that radiates peace and embraces all with love.

2. **Inner Examination for Truth's Alignment:** One can discern their allegiance—whether to Truth or self—by examining their thoughts, emotions, and actions. Do they harbor suspicions, enmities, or desires born of selfishness? Those tendencies point to self-worship. Alternatively, if one fiercely combats these traits and embodies gentleness, unselfishness, and readiness to yield personal comforts for others, they incline toward Truth, irrespective of professed religious affiliations.

3. **Selfish Pursuits versus Detachment from Self:** Those ensnared by self-indulgence, seeking personal gain, power, and recognition, essentially serve their ego. On the contrary, those who renounce the craving for wealth, the urge for dominance, and the pursuit of personal accolades show signs of detachment from self, even if their religious expressions are minimal.

4. **Egoistic Pride versus Humble Demeanor:** The self-centered exude ostentation, strive for recognition, and often indulge in self-praise. Those who genuinely repress the urge to boast, are content with humility, and willingly take the lowest place without seeking attention, exhibit a detachment from self, aligning more closely with the essence of Truth regardless of their outward expressions of worship.

The signs by which the Truth-lover is known are unmistakable. Hear the Holy Krishna declare them, in Sir Edwin Arnold's beautiful rendering of the "Bhagavad Gita":—

"Fearlessness, singleness of soul, the will
Always to strive for wisdom; opened hand
And governed appetites; and piety,
And love of lonely study; humbleness,
Uprightness, heed to injure nought which lives
Truthfulness, slowness unto wrath, a mind
That lightly letteth go what others prize;
And equanimity, and charity
Which spieth no man's faults; and tenderness
Towards all that suffer; a contented heart,
Fluttered by no desires; a bearing mild,
Modest and grave, with manhood nobly mixed,
With patience, fortitude and purity;
An unrevengeful spirit, never given
To rate itself too high--such be the signs,
O Indian Prince! of him whose feet are set
On that fair path which leads to heavenly birth!"

In the vast labyrinth of confusion and self-absorption, when individuals drift away from the celestial essence of holiness and

Truth, they often resort to crafting subjective benchmarks to evaluate each other. They establish these benchmarks based on their distinct ideologies, making their own theological beliefs the ultimate litmus test for Truth. Consequently, humanity becomes fragmented, torn apart by divergent convictions, leading to perpetual discord, animosity, and an unrelenting cycle of anguish and hardship. This disconnection from a shared understanding of higher truth plunges people into ceaseless conflicts and divides, fostering an atmosphere of enduring sorrow and persistent suffering that seems unending.

As you delve into the quest for Truth, consider this: the singular path lies in the relinquishment of self. It requires the relinquishing of all those entrenched facets—be it the fervent desires, insatiable appetites, deeply rooted opinions, or the confinements of limited perceptions and biases—that have tightly gripped you thus far. Liberating yourself from these bonds is the gateway to embracing Truth. It demands shedding the shackles that have bound you, allowing these limitations to cascade away. As you do so, Truth will gradually reveal itself to you, unfurling its profound wisdom.

Challenge the notion that your faith or belief system reigns supreme above all others. Instead, cultivate a humble spirit that seeks to grasp the paramount lesson of compassion and goodwill toward all. Release the belief that your revered figure or deity is the sole redeemer, while dismissing the sincere devotion of others as fallacy. Rather, ardently pursue the path of purity and righteousness, and you will come to understand that every soul dedicated to holiness serves as a beacon of salvation for humanity. Embrace the understanding that every saintly individual contributes to the collective upliftment of mankind, transcending the confines of any singular doctrine or belief system.

The surrender of the self is a profound journey that transcends mere external renunciations. It goes beyond the abandonment of material possessions and superficial trappings. True renunciation involves shedding the internal vices, the inner fallacies that often entangle us. The path to Truth isn't paved solely by discarding extravagant attire, relinquishing wealth, abstaining from specific foods, or articulating eloquent phrases. Rather, it is found in shedding the spirit of conceit, in letting go of the relentless pursuit of riches, in refraining from the indulgence of self-centric desires.

Discovering Truth entails relinquishing all forms of animosity, discord, judgment, and ego-driven pursuits. It involves nurturing a heart that embodies gentleness and purity. It is not about performing external acts devoid of internal transformation; it's about internalizing the essence of selflessness and purity. Choosing the former without embracing the latter is akin to practicing hypocrisy—a mere semblance of righteousness. However, embracing the inner transformation inherently encompasses external renunciations.

One might isolate oneself from the external world, retreating to a cave or a remote forest, yet carry the burden of selfishness within. Without shedding this inner burden, the pursuit remains futile, leading to profound wretchedness and a distorted reality. Conversely, one can exist within the throes of worldly duties and responsibilities while renouncing the inner ego. True renunciation is about liberating oneself from the internal adversary—the ego and selfish desires.

To be in the world but not governed by its superficial trappings is the pinnacle of spiritual attainment. It signifies the ultimate conquest, attaining a state of supreme tranquility amidst the chaos—a victory that surpasses all others.

The renunciation of self is the way of Truth, therefore,

"Enter the Path; there is no grief like hate,
No pain like passion, no deceit like sense;
Enter the Path; far hath he gone whose foot
Treads down one fond offense."

1. **Perspective Clarification:** As one conquers the self, a profound shift in perception occurs. The sway of passions, biases, likes, and dislikes distorts reality, molding everything to fit within those limitations. However, a soul devoid of these biases sees with pristine clarity. Free from prejudice, it perceives itself and others accurately, recognizing the true essence beyond subjective biases.
2. **Harmonious Perception:** Such a liberated soul comprehends the world in its authentic proportions and rightful connections. It ceases to harbor the need for attack, defense, or concealment. This tranquil state allows a harmonious view of existence, fostering a profound peace within. This tranquility is the embodiment of Truth, a state untouched by the chaos of conflicting interests.
3. **Simplicity in Truth:** The unblemished state of mind and heart epitomizes the profound simplicity of Truth. This serene state signifies an absence of prejudice or preference, granting access to a blessed realm of existence. It's a state where one dwells among the celestial, seated in reverence before the Supreme.
4. **Understanding and Compassion:** Those attaining this state possess profound knowledge—the Great Law, the origin of sorrow, the path to liberation. Despite comprehending the world's blindness, immersed in its self-created illusions and ensnared in darkness,

they retain immense compassion. They understand that despite the world's current state, every soul will eventually return to the fold of Truth.
5. **Goodwill and Compassionate Outlook:** Hence, they dwell in goodwill toward all beings, viewing them with the tenderness of a loving father for his wayward children. Their gaze doesn't harbor condemnation or strife, but rather, it brims with a compassionate understanding of the journey each soul undertakes towards realization.
6. **Final Redemption:** They envision a future where, after ages of suffering, every lost soul shall seek solace in the final refuge of Truth. With patience and a far-reaching perspective, they await the eventual return of every wandering spirit to the embrace of ultimate Truth.

This journey entails a profound shift in perception, culminating in an enlightened state that fosters compassion, understanding, and an unwavering belief in the eventual redemption of all souls.

The comprehension of Truth eludes humanity due to their unwavering attachment to self. This staunch belief in and affection for the concept of self blinds individuals from perceiving the essence of Truth, tricking them into perceiving self as the sole reality—a fallacy that veils the actuality of existence.

However, the pivotal moment arrives when one relinquishes this deep-rooted faith in and fondness for the self. In that liberating moment, the ties to self dissolve, and the flight towards Truth commences. It is in this flight that one unearths the eternal Reality, transcending the confines of the illusory self.

Humanity often finds itself in a state of intoxication,

indulging in the allure of opulent luxuries, fleeting pleasures, and the vanity of worldly pursuits. Amidst this indulgence, the thirst for a meaningful existence intensifies, leading to self-deception—the illusion of an enduring bodily existence. Yet, when the inevitable harvest of their actions unfolds, pain and sorrow surface, shattering the illusions they once embraced.

In these moments of anguish and humility, stripped of all pretense and intoxicated illusions, individuals are forced to confront the stark reality. With hearts burdened by the weight of experiences, they relinquish the self and its intoxicating allure. In this surrender, they seek solace in the singular immortality—the spiritual realm of Truth that dismantles all falsehoods and delusions.

It's within this journey of disillusionment and relinquishment that one discovers the transcendental immortality—a realm beyond the ephemeral, where Truth reigns supreme, dispelling all illusions and offering a lasting refuge.

The journey from evil to good, from the confinement of self to the liberation of Truth, unfolds through the profound corridors of sorrow. This inherent link between sorrow and self intertwines their fates, binding them inseparably. However, it's within the tranquil embrace and euphoria of Truth that the omnipresence of sorrow is conquered and dissipated.

Consider moments of disappointment stemming from thwarted plans or unmet expectations, or the sting of remorse due to one's actions—the root lies in the attachment to self. Similarly, feeling aggrieved by someone's demeanor or words reflects the stronghold of self-centered thoughts. Even the wounds inflicted by others' deeds or words, causing deep hurt, are manifestations of traversing the arduous path of self.

Every facet of suffering originates from the fortress of self. Yet, therein lies the profound revelation—every suffering culminates in Truth. Upon entering and experiencing the profound depths of Truth, the grip of disappointment, remorse, regret, and the very essence of sorrow fades away. This immersion in Truth signifies an emancipation from the shackles of suffering, where sorrow finds no refuge within.

Ultimately, the realization of Truth marks the end of suffering's reign. Disappointment, regret, remorse, and the very essence of sorrow dissipate in the radiance of Truth, leaving behind a liberated soul untouched by the shadows of self-imposed suffering.

> *"Self is the only prison that can ever bind the soul;*
> *Truth is the only angel that can bid the gates unroll;*
> *And when he comes to call thee, arise and follow fast;*
> *His way may lie through darkness, but it leads to light at last."*

The profound truth resonates in the understanding that much of the world's woe is an outcome of its own actions and choices. In this intricate tapestry of existence, sorrow plays a transformative role—it acts as a refining agent, purging impurities and instilling depth within the soul. Moreover, the pinnacle of sorrow serves as the precursor to the revelation of Truth.

Reflect upon your experiences: Have you traversed through substantial suffering? Have you delved into the depths of profound sorrow, allowing it to carve profound insights into your being? Have you dedicated genuine contemplation to the enigmatic riddle of life's purpose and essence? If your journey has embraced these trials, it signifies readiness—a preparedness to engage in the relentless battle against self, marking the initiation as a disciple of Truth.

Suffering, when deeply felt and earnestly contemplated,

becomes a catalyst for transformation. It acts as a catalyst propelling one towards a newfound understanding and readiness to confront the illusions of self. This state of readiness heralds the commencement of a profound journey—a quest to dismantle the veils of self-delusion and embrace the teachings of Truth.

The scholars and intellectuals, engrossed in their intellectual pursuits, often construct intricate theories about the universe, labeling them as the ultimate Truth. However, there lies a distinct path—one that diverges from mere theoretical contemplation. It beckons you to embark upon the direct route of righteous action, transcending the boundaries of mere speculation. It is on this path that Truth reveals itself—an entity not confined to theoretical constructs, steadfast and unwavering amidst the flux of ideologies.

Direct your focus towards nurturing your heart—a garden in need of continual cultivation. Bathe it in the perennial stream of selfless love and profound compassion. Strive ardently to expel any thoughts or emotions that diverge from the essence of Love. Uphold the practice of repaying malevolence with kindness, countering hatred with love, responding to cruelty with gentleness, and maintaining silence in the face of attack. In these actions lies the alchemical process—transforming the base elements of selfish desires into the purest essence of Love, consequently dissipating the illusion of self and unveiling the irrefutable Truth.

By walking this path, you'll traverse among humanity, free from blame, wearing the cloak of humility. You'll be harnessed not by the burdensome yoke of pride but rather by the effortless yoke of modesty. Your attire will not be the garb of arrogance but rather the divine vestment of humbleness, paving the way for self to merge seamlessly into the realm of Truth.

"O come, weary brother! thy struggling and striving
End thou in the heart of the Master of ruth;
Across self's drear desert why wilt thou be driving,
Athirst for the quickening waters of Truth
When here, by the path of thy searching and sinning,
Flows Life's gladsome stream, lies Love's oasis green?
Come, turn thou and rest; know the end and beginning,
The sought and the searcher, the seer and seen.
Thy Master sits not in the unapproached mountains,
Nor dwells in the mirage which floats on the air,
Nor shalt thou discover His magical fountains
In pathways of sand that encircle despair.
In selfhood's dark desert cease wearily seeking
The odorous tracks of the feet of thy King;
And if thou wouldst hear the sweet sound of His speaking,
Be deaf to all voices that emptily sing.
Flee the vanishing places; renounce all thou hast;
Leave all that thou lovest, and, naked and bare,
Thyself at the shrine of the Innermost cast;
The Highest, the Holiest, the Changeless is there.
Within, in the heart of the Silence He dwelleth;
Leave sorrow and sin, leave thy wanderings sore;
Come bathe in His Joy, whilst He, whispering, telleth
Thy soul what it seeketh, and wander no more.
Then cease, weary brother, thy struggling and striving;
Find peace in the heart of the Master of ruth.
Across self's dark desert cease wearily driving;
Come; drink at the beautiful waters of Truth.

www.ingramcontent.com/pod-product-compliance
Lightning Source LLC
Chambersburg PA
CBHW020848160426
43192CB00007B/836